Saturday, October 14, 2023

"IT'S TIME TO FLEE"

*Now when they had gone, behold, an angel of the Lord appeared to
Joseph in a dream and said, "Get up! Take the Child and His mother and flee ..... Matthew 2:13*

Scripture taken from the NEW AMERICAN STANDARD BIBLE,

Copyright 1960, 1962, 1963, 1968, 1971, 1972, 1975,1977, 1995 by the Lockman Foundation, Used by permission.

All Rights Reserved

ISBN: 979-8338593356 PB

979-8315639688 HB

Dedication

With love to Dennis, my faithful husband and partner in adventure.

You have shown me a whole new world.

And home is wherever you are.

Acknowledgment

This story exists because our dear friends Joan and Mike Sahl decided before we did that we needed to be volunteer guides at the Garden Tomb in Jerusalem. Thank you for pushing us to expand our territory. You really started something wonderful.

Thank you to past GT Director Steven Bridge who decided to take a chance and invite two inexperienced Americans to serve in that very special place. Also, thank you to the present GT Director Simon Holland and his wife Ann who lead all who work there with love and wisdom. Thank you for continually exhibiting wisdom and grace. We learn so much from you.

Thank you to our sons, Andy and Philip, who can't believe their parents are running all over the world and sometimes shake their heads in disbelief. We will love you unconditionally for the rest of our lives. Thank you to our daughter-in-law Nancy for loving us, praying so diligently for us and putting us in contact with our ex-Navy Seal friend that was so helpful when we needed him. We adore you.

Grandchildren Gracie, Mollie, Betsy, Thompson, Hays, Blakely, Maggie, Mason, Dax, Tiki, Gabby, great grandchildren Brooks and Hazel, I want you to know that we love each of you and are cheering you on from the stands. Jesus is the answer to all your questions. Life is found in Him.

Thank you to our extended family and to friends that have become family for always encouraging us and insisting this story be written.

Contents

Dedication ii

Acknowledgment iii

About the Author 1

Preface 2

PART I 3

CIRCUMSTANTIAL PEACE 3

Saturday, September 9, 2023 3

Sunday, September 10, 2023 9

Monday, September 11, 2023 10

Tuesday, September 12, 2023 13

Wednesday, September 13, 2023 15

Thursday, September 14, 2023 17

Friday, September 15, 2023 19

Saturday, September 16, 2023 21

Sunday, September 17, 2023 23

Monday, September 18, 2023 24

Tuesday, September 19, 2023 26

Wednesday, September 20, 2023 28

Thursday, September 21, 2023 30

Friday, September 22, 2023 32

Saturday, September 23, 2023 34

Sunday, September 24, 2023 36

Monday, September 25, 2023 37

Tuesday, September 26, 2023 38

Wednesday, September 27, 2023 40

Thursday, September 28, 2023 42

Friday, September 29, 2023 44

Saturday, September 30, 2023 46

Sunday, October 1, 2023 48

Monday, October 2, 2023 50

Tuesday, October 3, 2023 51

Wednesday, October 4, 2023 52

Thursday, October 5, 2023 54

Friday, October 6, 2023 55

PART II 57

WAR 57

Supernatural Peace 57

October 7, 2023 57

Sunday, October 8, 2023 60

Monday, October 9, 2023 62

Tuesday, October 10, 2023 64

Wednesday, October 11, 2023 66

Thursday, October 12, 2023 69

v

Friday, Oct 13, 2023 71

Saturday, October 14, 2023 73

Sunday, October 15, 2023 79

Monday, October 16, 2023 81

Tuesday, October 17, 2023 83

Wednesday, October 18, 2023 84

Thursday, October 19, 2023 86

Friday, October 20, 2023 88

Saturday, October 21, 2023 89

End of January 2024 90

End of February 2024 91

About the Author

Sharon Thompson Braner grew up in her grandparents' home in the small village of Concord, Illinois. She first heard about Jesus at the local Methodist Church as a child. After marrying her high school sweetheart, the young couple moved to Augusta, Georgia, and their life of adventure began. Following her husband's aviation career around the United States, she served as a Bible Teacher in various churches and as a Teaching Leader for Bible Study Fellowship in Little Rock, AR, Dallas, TX, and Savannah, GA. She has participated in Stonecroft Ministries as a speaker and chair and has enjoyed various mission trips. Dennis and Sharon never dreamed that one day they would be living and sharing the gospel with people from all nations in Jerusalem, Israel. They have two sons, nine grandchildren, and two great-grandchildren. Their adventures include extensive travel around the world. They now call Frisco, TX, home and serve in various positions at Stonebriar Community Church. She is also active in a vibrant Sewing Group and feisty Book Club.

Preface

"On October 7, 2023, Hamas terrorists kidnapped 251 people: men, women, and children from more than 20 nations. 50 were children and teens, including 2 babies, and 12 were under the age of 10."   Genesis Foundation 123

Thousands of people were shot, raped, mutilated and burned alive. The torture was demonic.

The following story is the true account of my husband and me volunteering in Jerusalem during the fall of 2023. Everyone who was present in the country at that time has a story of where they were, what they were doing, and how they were affected by the actions of terrorists on that horrific day.

Our story pales in comparison to so many others.

In the past 77 years there have been many wars fought in that tiny country. Adults and children alike know how to calmly run to bomb shelters when the Air Raid sirens blare, sometimes daily. We in American cannot relate. We have come to love the courage, resilience and bravery of all who call that very special country home.

We pray there will never be another October 7th.

We will return to Jerusalem. We will once again welcome visitors to the Garden Tomb and tell them the life-giving story of Jesus of Nazareth. Only HE can provide the supernatural peace and strength needed to face the many battles of this life.

We hope to see you at the Garden Tomb in Jerusalem.

PART I

CIRCUMSTANTIAL PEACE

5 Weeks Earlier

Saturday, September 9, 2023

A friend and staff member from the Garden Tomb picked us up at the Crown Plaza Hotel, Tel Aviv, Israel, about noon today. We've been in this country a few days now, and have enjoyed a much-needed time of rest. That flight from Dallas is a killer! Jet lag is real, and we have learned to accept it and try to avoid all its consequences. What better place than the beautiful beaches of Tel Aviv? What a lovely beach vacation for four days.

Yesterday we walked the concrete path along the Mediterranean Sea to Jaffe, played in the sea, and enjoyed fabulous food at a café right on the water. I envisioned Peter looking at that same view when he visited Jaffe so long ago. It's time for me to review that story.

The Crown Plaza, located right on the beach, was "almost" like the comforts of our Texas home with comfy beds, plus great views and activities on the beach to keep us entertained. Watching men's volleyball was very exciting every day. There were games at all times of the day and night played out right before our very eyes. How do they survive hitting that ball with their heads day after day?

It's a 45-minute drive to Jerusalem. While our dear friend and Dennis, husband of 52 years, chatted in the front seat of the car, I had plenty of time to reflect upon past adventures and anticipate what is ahead for the next two months.

This will be our fourth time volunteering as guides at the Garden Tomb, located in East Jerusalem. It never gets old, and we still consider this opportunity an unexpected gift from God.

The adventure began in 2015 when I was encouraged by a dear friend to consider becoming a tour guide at the "Garden Tomb" when Dennis retired. I had never heard of such a thing nor imagined that we would be participating in such a ministry in a foreign country. My definition of retirement certainly did not include international travel or being away from our home in Dallas—or the grandkids—for months at a time.

Back then, I did the research and learned that the Garden Tomb is a small plot of land, just under two acres, situated very near the Damascus Gate, which is the main entrance into the Old City of Jerusalem. Very near this Israeli Holy Site is a stone quarry that was used in Roman times as a place of execution. Inside the gated garden is an ancient wine press, which proves that the garden was once a vineyard. Within the vineyard is an ancient tomb that some Christians believe to be the very tomb of Jesus Christ.

It's good for me to review the particulars of this special place because I'll be repeating them many times over the next two months.

Thousands of tourists from all over the world travel to Jerusalem each year to visit the places where Jesus walked, talked, died, and rose again. The trip is often called the Pilgrimage to the Holy Lands. The Garden Tomb is always listed as one of the sights to see.

Our first visit to the Land of the Bible was in 2006 on a tour organized by Zola Levitt from Dallas. It was a fabulous experience with dear longtime friends and forty other newly found friends aboard the "Red Bus." We ran where Jesus walked and visited Caesarea, Tiberius, the Dead Sea, Masada, the Golan Heights, Gethsemane, the Mount of Olives, the Old City of Jerusalem, and all points in between. We tacked on a trip to Petra, Jordan, to see the famous *Treasury of Indiana Jones* fame. It was *the* trip of a lifetime.

We soaked it all in. Every spot held a memory, a scripture, a prayer, and a moment of worship. We loved it. Those memories are a source of happiness now, especially since our friend Jim is no longer with us. His memorial service a few months ago reminded us of how important adventures with loved ones can be.

The end of that trip was spent with an afternoon at the Garden Tomb in East Jerusalem. Of all the memories of our adventure that day, the time spent in the Garden was the most memorable. The older British gentleman who served as our guide explained that the rock face of Skull Hill could be the "place of the skull" mentioned in the scriptures where Jesus was led to be crucified. (*They took Jesus, therefore, and He went out bearing His own cross to the place called the Place of a Skull, which is called in Hebrew, Golgotha.* John 19:17) He shared the history of the many poor souls who died by crucifixion along the intersection of Damascus Road and Jericho Road. At that time, wooden crosses were placed at eye level so people walking by would see up close the horror of what might happen to them if they disobeyed the law.

We stood in awe, staring at that stone quarry, letting our imaginations take us back 2,000 years. We made our way through the Garden and down to the ancient tomb. (*Now in the place where He was crucified, there was a garden, and in the garden a new tomb in which no one had yet been laid. Therefore, because of the Jewish day of preparation, since the tomb was nearby, they laid Jesus there.* John 19:41-42) We bent down to crawl into the darkness and spent a few moments inside that rock cave, declaring it to be empty! If this were not the actual place of those events, it should have been. It has all the necessary parts mentioned in scripture.

Our gentleman guide was loving and kind and gave the most succinct presentation of the Gospel of Jesus Christ. I was so impressed with him. Our group shared communion at one of the many worship places in the Garden. It was the perfect ending to our Pilgrimage before returning to the United States.

After that trip, reading and studying the Bible became a brand-new experience. Those places were seared into our minds' eye and caused the Scriptures to come alive as we cherished mental visions of those very sites.

A few years later, we returned as tourists again. That trip was organized by our eldest son and included our teenage grandson! What a delight! We joined two other couples as makeshift chaperones of seventeen teenagers. That, too, was a wonderful experience. Those teenagers shot off those buses at each holy site like rockets, while the adults lumbered along behind, trying to catch up. Again, the trip was concluded with a visit to the Garden Tomb.

So, when my church friend suggested we might actually work there during retirement, it was an intriguing thought. After reading all about the site on their webpage, I clicked on the "volunteer here" button —and the unbelievable happened. After e-mails, conversations, more emails, references, filling out forms, and even more emails, two years after that first click, we received an email from the Director inviting us to come to

Jerusalem to serve as tour guides at the Garden Tomb for one month, to see if we liked them and they liked us. We were beyond surprised that this was actually going to happen.

We said yes! We scheduled a time months in advance and proceeded to pack.

After our first time serving there, studying, guiding, praying, and befriending other volunteers from all over the world, we were invited back, again and again.

And here we are, racing down that foreign highway once again toward our home away from home for the fourth time. The land is dry, the foliage parched, and the stone buildings are to gleam in the hot sunshine. We are scheduled to stay for eight weeks this time. We left home, family, convenience, and comfort of life in the United States to live in a little apartment located in a two-acre garden in the middle of the Muslim part of town, East Jerusalem, Israel. How crazy is that!

We are both so very excited. We will be reunited with friends and places we've grown to love, and will greet people from many countries, races, and creeds to share with them the greatest news of all time: Jesus lived, died, and rose again, all because He loved us. What a privilege to speak those words to hundreds of people every day. The response of visitors is always amazing and life-altering.

10 a.m.

We've arrived.

After some gentle teasing about the amount of luggage I brought, we unloaded at the Garden Tomb gate and were met by the unofficial welcoming committee. We smiled and hugged the Director and his lovely wife, along with several volunteers we'd grown to love from past experiences, and proceeded to settle into our apartment. What a lovely reunion. What a peaceful place.

We've been assigned different apartments each year we've been there, but this one was different. All stone apartments are located on the property, out of sight of visitors, and all are very adequate. Most are one-bedroom units, a living room/dining room combo, a kitchen, and a bath. But this year, we'd been assigned a newly renovated apartment that had a washing machine right there in the kitchen. That amenity was unheard of and never expected. My life would be much easier this year! I was thrilled. In past years we shared a washing machine with all the other volunteers. It was located down a few flights of stairs in a separate little building. We never did figure out how to work those machines; our laundry was always dripping wet as we hauled it up several flights of stairs to the rooftop lines to dry, but not this time. Joy of joys!

Volunteer friends from Dallas purchased a crockpot while they were there a few months ago and left it with instructions to have it ready for us when we arrived. What a luxury! I can't cook from scratch every day without a crockpot. We learned that the "proper" name for this appliance is "slow cooker" and that only "crackpots" use crockpots! Another amenity that will make my life easier.

After unpacking, we wandered down the ancient stone street outside the entrance of the site to the tiny local grocery store and reunited with its Greek Orthodox owner, his sons, and grandchildren. Oh, my…nothing had changed. The shelves are still stacked to the ceiling with minimal organization, Muslim women in their burqas were crowded and pushed their way down the tiny aisles, which were covered with all sorts of loose cardboard, boxes of inventory, and more people. After the confusion of the "checkout line", I made my purchase from the elderly owner. He informed me, "55 shekels!" I only had 50! "No worries, next time," he said, waving me out the door. He knew I'd be back often with a special request, and he would shout something in Arabic, and then a son would climb up mountains of cereal boxes, sauces, cookies, coffee, etc., and hand me the item I'd requested. What a system!

Nablus Road had not changed either. Lining the street are outdoor vegetable markets filled with beautiful produce, eggs, and fruit, along with an odd assortment of paraphernalia you might see at a Dollar General store in the States.

Fake Nike sneakers, toys, mounds of candy, drink stands, breads piled high, and the smell of roasting meat on skewers over open fires all challenged my senses. Smoke from the outdoor fires filled the air. Yep, we were "home." Burqa-clad Muslim women, men shouting in Arabic, children on scooters, and young men on motorbikes filled the outdoor space. This culture is far removed from that of Dallas, Texas.

Back at the apartment, we organized our cupboards and fridge, then took a short rest before joining the other volunteers and staff for the bimonthly dinner out together. We met at the gate and took a quick walk through the crowded Muslim streets to a favorite hotel that welcomed us to a feast. It was a wonderful evening of laughter, stories, and good but foreign food. We collapsed in bed.

Sunday, September 10, 2023

After a fitful, jet-lagged night, on Sunday morning, we walked a few blocks to board the light rail train that would carry us up the hill to the City Hall Center. We walked halfway back down the hill to Christ's Church, the oldest Protestant church in the Middle East. (Riding up the hill and walking halfway down was a lesson we'd learned in prior years.) It is our "home away from home" church while we live in Jerusalem. It had not changed either, and we saw beautiful, familiar faces and sang hymns in English and Hebrew. Communion is always very meaningful, and the service lasted its usual two hours. We knelt at the altar near people from various countries and received the broken bread in our outstretched palms, then dipped it in the chalice of wine. The pastor whispered those precious words, "This is MY body, broken for you," to each person. It's always an emotional time.

After visiting with friends in the courtyard after church, we walked through Jerusalem's city streets to our favorite IWO Armenian butcher shop about a mile away. Again, we were delighted with the bacon, hamburger, cheese, spaghetti, and sauces that were available. We learned that the sales tax in Israel is 17%, but we did not hesitate to spend about $300 to stock up our refrigerator. The very best bacon in the world is $50 a pound. It's a treat we can never forgo! We walked back to the light rail train and rode it down the hill to Damascus Gate, our stop, where we wound our way through the Muslim bus stop and all the sights and sounds back to our apartment. We did some laundry in the washing machine in the kitchen and hung it out on the lines to dry on our rooftop patio. Our simple, peaceful life in Jerusalem had begun. Much of our time would be spent walking to various shops for the necessities of life. I wonder how hard life must be for the neighboring Muslim women right around the corner and the Jewish women a few blocks over.

Today is our granddaughter Gracie's birthday and she celebrated at a lake in TX with her friends. We miss our family terribly but are focused on our work which will begin tomorrow.

Dennis is keeping up with his part-time job on his computer, staying in touch with his airplane deals and friends. I think it provides a sense of normalcy for him. It's quiet here tonight.

Monday, September 11, 2023

Mark 1:1-8

"Make ready the way of the Lord, Make His path straight."

Mark 1:3b

In ancient days a messenger would go before the King to prepare for His arrival. That task would include preparing the road <u>and</u> the people. John the Baptist called the people to repent for Jesus Christ the Lord, Jehovah God would soon arrive. Are the hearts of people today ready to receive the King? Is my heart ready?

Still very aware of jet lag I woke up at 5 am ready to go. After a shower and a slight case of vertigo we headed to the staff room for morning devotions.

Devotion time with the permanent staff and group of volunteers is my favorite time of day. We begin each day with worship led by one of the very talented leaders on their guitar or keyboard. Singing together is righteous, sincere, and glorious. Our undivided focus on Jesus strengthens us for each day's challenges. The Director read the scripture and applied it to our lives. We're studying the book of Mark this time. It is wonderful teaching.

The director asked me to prepare teaching for a week, beginning Oct 16, so I am studying during my free time, preparing homiletics, etc. Digging into the scriptures is my favorite pastime.

We are reminded daily that the Garden Tomb exists to provide a clear presentation of the gospel of Jesus, the most important need of every person. We pray that each one who enters the gate will experience the presence and power of the Lord during their visit. After prayer, we are dismissed with great smiles to "open the gate."

Hundreds of eager tourists line up along the alley leading to the gate every morning. Each group had made reservations for their time to be in the Garden. People from all nations are welcome, free of charge.

After devotions today, I stumbled back to the apartment for a nap. Jet lag is real, and our first shift to guide started at 12:30. I need to be ready, refreshed, and alert.

This year, the new director had arranged for the volunteers to work in four-hour shifts. HALLELUJAH! That is welcome news for this old lady. I'd been preparing for this very physical volunteer work for months back in Dallas by walking a mile or so every day, but still, I realized this chick was aging! And this "job" is strenuous.

My first group was 350 Americans. What a joy! They spoke Texan, and we got along just fine.

They were wide-eyed at Skull Hill, listening carefully to the fulfillment of the bloody Old Testament sacrifices. They were facing the rock-faced hill called Calvary or Golgotha, and as always, it is a commanding sight for first-time visitors.

They took pictures of the carved marble plaque that rests near the marble bleachers where they sat.

"They took Jesus, therefore, and he went out, bearing His own cross to the place called the Place of a Skull, which is called in Hebrew, Golgotha. John 19:17

I will repeat that verse hundreds of times.

They took many more pictures of the quarry, and all stood in awe. We walked down the stone path into the garden and sat on the white stone benches. They were very quiet as I explained the significance of the history of the fact that grapes were harvested in that very place. The present-day olive trees and beautiful flowers are a modern-day addition to what was once a very productive vineyard owned by a wealthy man in the area, perhaps Joseph of Arimathea. The ancient winepress was of particular interest to every visitor. More pictures.

We walked down the worn stone steps to the tomb itself, and a few folks at a time entered that holy cave. I told them as I tell all the pilgrims, they have come a long way to see nothing. On a Sunday over 2000 years ago Mary Magdalene and her friends were just as astonished to see the stone slab empty and hear the voice of the living Jesus in the garden.

There were tears flowing, smiles all around, singing, and more pictures taken of this life-changing experience.

After they were situated on marble benches for their worship and communion time together, I returned to the front gate and was assigned a new group. These new friends were from Tanzania and spoke only Swahili. I told the story of the gospel of Jesus with the help of a pitiful, smiling interpreter.

Somehow, we communicated, and they left smiling, too. They were beautiful believers, and their singing in the garden during their worship time was beautiful.

Dennis led two groups from Louisiana and Tennessee. He flourishes in the guiding position, loving every minute of it and making friends quickly and easily.

Construction on the tomb approach is happening. This new renovation will provide an orderly and safe entrance as crowds of people wait their turn to see the emptiness. The men using jackhammers are careful to stop the noise when pilgrims approach. Volunteers and guides stepping over construction materials is not safe, and we watch everyone closely to prevent falls.

We ended the day with chicken and noodles and the famous Israeli cucumber salad.

We played a few games of chess and texted friends and family. Staying in touch with people we love helps stave off the homesickness. We are missing granddaughter Mollie's volleyball games, but try to watch them online.

The crockpot is on low overnight.

Tuesday, September 12, 2023

Mark 1:9-13

"You are My beloved Son, in You I am well-pleased."

Mark 1:11b

The Spirit came upon Jesus when He was baptized, and a voice from heaven declared Him to be the beloved Son of the Heavenly Father. This God Man was truly God the Son. Who do people say Jesus is? Do I proclaim Him as Deity here in this place? Do visitors realize who He is?

Exhaustion is still a problem, so I slept in and skipped devotions, thinking just a few more hours of sleep would help. Much to my surprise, as soon as I closed my eyes once again for a much-needed morning nap, the hammering and drilling started as construction on the tomb approach began for the day. I should've known better. It usually takes me five days before jet lag is gone and I feel like a human being again. Time is the only cure for this physical issue. I'm afraid I lean toward frustration rather than patience in the meantime.

Later in the morning, we walked to the tiny pharmacy, winding through the Muslim population on the street, to get some distilled water to try to flush the dust from my nose and sinuses with a neti pot I'd brought from home. Dust is everywhere; this city is located in a desert, after all. Every effort taken to prevent sinus trouble is important.

Back at the garden, we met a local volunteer who had been added to the roster. She is a lovely elderly lady devoted to prayer. What a treasure of wisdom, love, and kindness. I know we are going to become great friends. Her lovely smile exudes the peace that characterizes her life.

Our shift started at 12:30 again, and larger groups were scheduled. The Garden is buzzing with people, which is such an answer to prayer. The memory of being closed during the COVID-19 pandemic years is still fresh in everyone's mind. That was a very trying time, and visitors were rare. Now, there is much welcome chatter and joy on those worn stones throughout that two-acre plot of land.

It was a good day greeting people from all over the world, listening to their singing, and watching their smiles as they exited the ancient tomb while declaring, "It's empty!" Forgiveness and reconciliation to the Heavenly Father bring a soul peace that unbelievers cannot comprehend. It is celebrated in this place many times, day after day.

Again, if this area is not the place of the death, burial, and resurrection of Jesus of Nazareth, it should have been. We have all the parts! It is truly a beautiful visual aid, and the tourists will never read their Bible the same again.

We ended the day exhausted again.

Wednesday, September 13, 2023

Mark 1:14-20

"Follow Me and I will make you fishers of men."

Mark 1:17

"Fishers of men" was not a new phrase coined by Jesus. Other teachers often used "bait" to "catch" men in their way of thinking. Fishermen knew the meaning of hard work, patience, and tenacity. Jesus called Simon and Andrew to leave their fishing nets, for He had a greater career designed for them. Seven of the disciples were former fishermen. The obedient eleven disciples changed the world. I'm wondering what I've been fishing for lately.

Good news from our Texas friends arrived via text. The Women's Bible Study at the church that I normally teach back in Frisco, TX., has begun, and 60 women have registered. I'm thrilled. We chose a new study, The Sermon on the Mount, with a great teacher, and the ladies are responding positively. I miss them already, but I will try to keep up with them in the study here by myself.

The tomb entrance construction is still a mess, but plants are being placed around the stones, and people are deciding if they like the new design. Even positive change is hard, but all the changes are going to allow more people access to the tomb entrance in an orderly fashion. Several construction workers brought mattresses and blankets and will spend nights in the Emmaus Chapel (the newly renovated chapel underground) in order to be on site early each day. They work so hard. We smile and nod at them as we pass by, wishing we could speak their language.

One of the volunteers has suffered terribly from mosquito bites all over her face. I'm so glad I brought the powerful mosquito spray from the US. She's had to go to the doctor for the swelling. She's so miserable. Dr. John provides good care for the volunteers when something like that arises. Daily problems of life still arise among the staff and volunteers and must be handled between shifts.

We were very busy today. Dennis led 180 Norwegian teenagers around and loved every minute of it. They were delightful. I served as a prayer guide, wandering around the property looking for people sitting alone. I had a great conversation with a young Jewish man who is now interested in Jesus. He had so many questions, and it was refreshing to see his genuine interest in the Messiah. I wonder if the Lord is drawing that young man to Himself.

Other volunteer guides led many groups as well, and the Garden was full of activity.

We ended the day exhausted. We hung the laundry on lines on the patio to dry just as the Muslim call to prayer began.

Thursday, September 14, 2023

Mark 1:21-34

"He was teaching them as One having authority."

Mark 1:22

Jesus spoke with authority, but not as one engaged in the political realm. The Kingdom of God involves His reign over the lives of His people. To become a citizen of His kingdom, one must believe the Good News of the Gospel and be born again. Do I share the Gospel with His authority every single time?

Our chauffeur and the Garden Tomb shop director led devotions this morning. His Ukrainian accent and perspective are delightful. He always chooses the most insignificant lines of scripture and develops them into practical and wonderful applications. Singing and praying with these people is a foretaste of heaven. These folks love and live for the Lord. They are not perfect people, but they are very focused. We end our time each day with extended silent prayer; what a holy time. We are united and a picture of the family of God.

The people working here are professional people, pastors, pastors' wives, young career women, retired school teachers, etc., all joined together for one purpose. Many speak several languages to greet guests from all over the world in their native tongue. Sadly, we speak only Texan. What a diverse team.

This morning, we prepared communion for 450 people from 8:30 – 12:30. The "kitchen" very near the entrance gate stores all communion supplies, and that's where the work begins. Small Olive wood or plastic cups are carefully filled with chilled grape juice, and the matzo bread is broken into small pieces and counted for the number of people in each group. Silver communion trays are available. A note of welcome written in the specific language of each group is selected, and all is covered with a lace cloth to remind people of the significance and holiness of the "bread and wine." The elements are then carried to the appropriate location to be ready when the group arrives. That involves a lot of walking! When we are assigned to this task, my apple watch tells me that I walk 5 miles a day. How is that even possible?

Delivering communion throughout the Garden means hearing worship songs sung in many different languages all at once as I walk by the meeting places. I can tell by the tune what hymn is being sung even though I cannot understand the words. Surely, that is what heaven will sound like when people from all nations and tongues will praise Jesus as they sing around the heavenly throne.

We took a nap after lunch and made plans to meet our Italian "son" at Notre Dame Restaurant this evening. This young man was our neighbor at the Garden Tomb apartments last spring. At that time, we shared watermelon and pizza, laughed, and listened to his dreams. He came to Dallas and stayed with us for a week last December. We've kept up with him throughout the year. We adore him, and he thinks of us as his American parents. His bright smile and love for the Lord are so refreshing.

We walked up the hill to the Notre Dame Catholic complex through the back alleys of Jewish homes and he arrived on his new motor bike. What a delightful evening. He shared the news of his new apartment and new job at the King of Kings Church in Jerusalem. He leads worship and a youth group. He is dating and seems very happy. We are so proud of him.

After dinner, we walked back down the hill and noticed an unusually heavy military presence. Rosh Hashanah has begun, and the barricades are ready for any trouble between the Muslims and Jews that might arise. The season of Jewish holidays has started. Skirmishes are always possible in this land of tension, but actual violence on this night seems impossible. We feel very safe walking these unfamiliar alleys even after dark.

It's cooled off, the windows of our apartment are open for the night and the A/C is finally shut off. The Muslim call to prayer will start again at 4 a.m. We can see the minaret speaker towering over our apartments from the patio, it's too close.

Friday, September 15, 2023

Mark 1:35-45

"Moved with compassion, Jesus stretched out His hand and touched him."

Mark 1:41

The faith of the leper is to be admired. He knew Jesus could heal him, he just had to ask. It was only a touch but a powerful divine touch that brought instant healing. That's how Jesus works, isn't it? Instantaneous forgiveness, life, purpose, love, and freedom. Just instantaneous. He's still in the business of healing the broken lives and hearts of people who come into the Garden.

Another lovely volunteer led devotions this morning. She is the devoted wife of a retired English vicar. It was wonderful. She explained the scripture word for word as we continued our study of the book of Mark. We are great friends. She and her husband are delightful. He has a great sense of quick humor and keeps us laughing. We hang around them as much as possible, making memories. Oh, to be neighbors with this fine couple from the UK, perhaps in heaven one day.

It's been a pretty slow day only 800 folks through the gate. But those that came heard the story. It's such a privilege to tell it again and again.

We had a quick BLT (love that American food) after work and met others at the gate for a walk to the Western Wall. Rosh Shoshana has begun, and we were curious to see the action going on down at the wall. We walked through the Damascus Gate, through the Muslim cardo. Even in the evening, the shops are open for tourists to buy souvenirs, food, and trinkets of every kind. The shops are deep, and treasures abound. Muslim men sit on their little chairs outside their shops, urging tourists to come in and buy their goods. They are very aware we are Americans from Dallas; they can spot us a mile away.

The sights and smells are unforgettable. The narrow stone pathway is always very crowded with interesting people from every nation.

We watched and waited at the Western Wall for a while. Many Jews were praying, nodding, and reading but no priestly blessing tonight. It is Shabbat, we heard the siren announcing its arrival before sundown. It's the same procedure every Friday night.

Military presence is always near as we walked uphill back through the shops and shoppers. Another normal peaceful evening in Jerusalem.

Saturday, September 16, 2023

Mark 2:1-12

"We have never seen anything like this."

Mark 2:12b

Jesus healed the paralytic so that those witnessing the miracle would know that He was the Son of Man and had the authority to forgive sins. Which is greater for Jesus, to forgive? Or to heal? Which is the greater need? Who but God can forgive? The people were stunned and glorifying God. So many people are in need of freedom from guilt through His forgiveness. Who can explain such a supernatural gift available to all who believe?

This morning, we did laundry (again) in the washing machine in the kitchen, what a luxury! We hung things out to dry on the racks on the patio adjoining our room. We share that area with another couple that are in the apartment next to us. We live very close together and it works just fine. Daily chores take on a new importance and more time because no task is as easy as it is in Texas.

We learned that the priestly blessing at the Western Wall was held at 1 a.m. Today, all the roads in the Jewish area are blocked and empty. There is no traffic, no shops open, and no Jewish men, women, or children in the streets. The Arab areas are still open with chaos everywhere, as usual.

We walked into the Old City though the Damascus Gate again looking for a store that resembles a mini-Kroger, with brands we can recognize. There are so many alleys of ancient stone.

We twisted around and around, asking shop owners where the "market" was located. We got several different directions and then just happened upon it. This market was recommended by other Dallas volunteers who stumbled onto it when they were here last spring. It's almost a normal supermarket! It's very small but clean and stocked in an orderly fashion. Unlike most markets, there are firm prices printed on every item. We found crackers, mayonnaise, and a few other items we recognized. Hallelujah! It's the little discoveries that make mealtimes happy here.

This afternoon we met church members of Prestonwood Baptist Church of Plano Texas in the Garden. We meet people from Dallas regularly. It's a welcome sight! We've heard it said that, eventually, everyone ends up in Jerusalem!

I am studying Mark chapters 8 & 9, getting ready to reach Oct 16th. Since there is no TV, Radio, or other distractions, studying is a welcome joy. I'm very thankful for the Bible Study Fellowship training of over 20 years that gave me a love of analyzing passages until they make sense to me and provide a personal application. Sharing with the staff and volunteers here is a wonderful opportunity, I am so humbled and excited.

Sunday, September 17, 2023
No devotions this morning.

It was a cool morning, and we slept in. Perhaps jet lag is lingering.

We walked up the hill to New Gate, down through the Christian/Catholic quarter to Christs Church. Rosh Shoshana is still being celebrated so all the Jewish roads are empty.

The church's pastor is back from Edinburgh, so it was wonderful to be at Christ's Church. We reunited with old friends and enjoyed being "home." He remembered us from previous years.

After church, we stayed for a tour and a history of the church with another young pastor. Very interesting.

We walked over to Manila Mall, thinking we'd have a wonderful lunch there, but everything was closed. There was nothing to do but walk back down the hill to the "Olive," the Muslim restaurant that opened last spring when we were here. It was all fresh and new and delicious then, even if we never ever received what we ordered. The Arab food is still fabulous, but the restaurant looks tired and old. The Hookah Bar is still available for the burqa-clad young women who seem to love smoking that mess.

Back at the apartment, we ZOOMED the Marathon on Sunday
The School Class gave them a brief report and then watched Pastor Chuck Swindoll's sermon, "Guilt or Grace," on Dennis's laptop. Technology keeps us close to our beloved church, Stonebriar Community Church of Frisco, TX.

Monday, September 18, 2023
Mark 2:13-17

"Why is He eating with tax collectors and sinners?"
Mark 2:16b

Why would Jesus not eat with the despised? He loved them and gave Himself for them while they were yet sinners. Oh, me too! All have sinned and fallen short of the glory of God, and it's been said that the ground at the cross is level. Who do I consider despised? Can I see the image of God in people who don't look like me?

Our alarm didn't go off, so we missed devotions this morning, but it wasn't long before the FIRE ALARM was blaring! That was a new experience! Everyone trudged down the stairs of their apartments or from wherever they were in the Garden, and we all met out in the alley. One-liners and lots of laughter started flying because there obviously was NOT a fire anywhere in the compound, and there we stood. Laughter is a common sound with these folks.

Back at the apartment all we could hear was construction workers on the roof. We both looked at each other at the same time and said, "Knock three times on the ceiling if you want me." Bless Tony Orlando!

Dennis spent the afternoon guiding, and I met with the director's wife to be officially trained to be a "prayer guide." Joy of Joys! I'd been hoping a position like this would be created for years. I felt that too many people were coming into the garden by themselves and needed attention. This position fits me like a glove.

After a lovely time with the director's wife, I walked through the Garden praying silently, looking for anyone who was sitting alone and not with a larger group. I met and prayed with a young couple from Waco, TX. They are transplants from Homestead Village outside Waco, TX, who have moved to Israel to establish a similar community north of Haifa, with about 120 people involved. She is pregnant with their first child, and they are very excited. What a lovely young couple, with fresh faces, smiling eyes, and godly conversation. They are planning a fall festival and have invited us to attend.

Today, our eldest son Andy connected us with the administrator to the Greek Orthodox Priest, "His Holy Beatitude." Yes, that's his title. Andy recently toured him around Washington, DC several times and knows him personally. This priest oversees part of the Church of the Holy Sepulcher. He's the guy in the long black robe, tall priestly hat, huge gold cross around his neck, a very long gray beard, and a serious expression. His assistant will give us a behind-the-scenes tour. To be able to meet this woman and hear her perspective gives us something wonderful to look forward to next week.

Tuesday, September 19, 2023

Mark 2:18-22

"But the days will come when the bridegroom will be taken away."
Mark 2:20a

Jesus stood before them in the flesh, the perfect Son of God. The opportunity to know Him, to touch Him, and to hear His audible voice was given to that generation. Yet His presence would soon be gone, and their lives would change dramatically. He filled them with all they needed to know at that moment. They actually saw the Lord. How I long to see Him face to face!

After devotions, I began the day as an official Prayer Guide. This position is wonderful. There's hardly anything I'd rather be doing. Today, I met a woman from the Netherlands, and we chatted a bit. Then, I sat down next to a Pastor and his wife, an Indian couple from Canada, who were simply delightful. We sat on the stone benches in front of the shop for a long time and reviewed the resurrection story. They became dear friends, we bonded together through the blood of Jesus. I may need to put these new friends on my Christmas Card List.

All cultures, colors, and creeds are united in the blood of Jesus. The church is alive and well all over the world. It's so encouraging to see these believers.

After the Garden closed for the day, we walked over to the Muslim market and purchased vegetables, again! It's always a challenge to buy what you see and not what's on the list. It's a colorful area of Nablus Road, with apples, oranges, pomegranates, onions, potatoes, greens of all flavors, eggs, huge cabbage, radishes, cilantro, etc. But I can never find celery!

Tonight, we "zoomed" our Texas church buddies. What a treat! One looked like she was sitting in a corn field, thanks to background technology, others were surrounded by and sitting on pumpkins. How fun to decorate for fall and Halloween in the States. We'll do nothing like that this year. That holiday doesn't exist in Jerusalem.

This year, we're going to celebrate the Jewish holidays that have been commemorated for thousands of years. It'll be a new experience.

Wednesday, September 20, 2023
Mark 2:23-28

"The Sabbath was made for man, and not man for the Sabbath."

Mark 2:27

Jesus broke the rules, the ones they'd been following since Leviticus was scratched down on the parchment scrolls. It was a hard pill to swallow. He fulfilled all the ceremonies and laws, including the Sabbath, for He Himself declared that the Son of Man is Lord of the Sabbath. He would heal and eat as He pleased, not as their law dictated. They had to rethink everything they'd been taught. How hard is it to rethink a long-held position?

This morning, we took the light rail to the Jewish Market and loaded up on groceries, again! Food shopping seems to be almost a daily chore for us and the locals. That's life here. We saw a Garden Tomb employee at the Shuk, the Jewish open-air market. Wow, how can that be? Of all the thousands of people running to and fro, we actually met someone we know. What fun!

The IWO butcher shop and IWO Hamburger restaurant are becoming our favorite places in all the Middle East. The guy at the butcher shop is getting to know us on a first name basis and is very friendly. He should be. We spend a fortune there.

The shop is exceptional and always clean and stocked with things we love and actually recognize. Never mind that bacon is still $50 a pound. We would never pay that in the States, but here, it is a luxury we cannot do without. We purchased spaghetti sauce, hamburger patties, ham slices, bacon, fancy bread, etc. We cannot get enough of this place. The burger restaurant in the next block is equally wonderful. We no longer have to miss a true American Hamburger. It's such a treat to have food that we recognize.

We spend SO much time wandering around, gathering food. There just is no "one stop shop" here. Maybe next time we come to Israel we'll find a real KROGER. Some volunteers call a market and have food delivered. That's next on my list of things to do.

After shopping, Dennis got a haircut at the Jewish barber shop, and we made our way back to East Jerusalem on the light rail to get ready for the big party tonight. I'm never brave enough to get my hair done here. I tell him he needs a Muslim or Jewish hairdo to blend in with the culture.

The construction of the new path to the tomb is complete, and it's celebration time. All the people and their families involved in the Garden Tomb were invited, and 150 folks attended. The catered bar-be-que was fabulous. Meats we recognized and desserts we didn't were on the lovely buffet set up in the garden itself. The Chairman of the Garden Tomb Trustee Board and his wife came from England to help us dedicate the new construction. They are wonderful, humble people. We visited with them and got to know them better. There was much singing, laughter, prayer, and love.

The lovely young Christian Palestinian woman that serves as CFO of the Garden came with her new baby boy. I gave her and another employee that just had a baby girl baby quilts that I made and brought from the US. They quietly smiled.

What a wonderful evening!

Thursday, September 21, 2023
Mark 3:1-6

"Is it lawful to do good or to do harm on the Sabbath, to save a life or to kill it? "
Mark 3:4

The Pharisees tried to trap Jesus into breaking a law so they could arrest Him and get rid of the threat He was bringing to their positions and authority. Fearlessly, He stood before them and healed the man's withered hand. They were no threat to Him, He was the Son of God after all. Unbelievers have crazy sometimes trick questions about Jesus, yet He wants to be made known.

Today is our first grandson's 25th birthday, and we are so far away. I'm praying he has a wonderful day. It's bizarre to be so far away from family. Never in a million years did I ever dream we'd be involved in an international ministry.

I woke up and realized I had lost my name badge and apartment keys! OH. NO. I confessed at devotions, and after some friendly teasing, I realized there would be no penalty, but only help to replace them.

My first group in the morning was a large group from Indonesia. No English! That's always the hardest part of guiding, but we made it through with lots of smiles and nods. They knew the story! We are always amazed at the love and dedication these people have for the Lord Jesus. They wept, sang hymns in their language, and enjoyed communion in one of the meeting places prepared just for them. I recognized the tune of the hymn but not the words, so I sang in English as I returned to the reception for another group to lead. The international church is alive and flourishing, even in countries where the people must meet "underground." Perhaps the church is even stronger in those places where it is being persecuted.

After lunch, we searched and cleaned the apartment from top to bottom. No keys or badge. The administrator in charge of these things knows of my dilemma. He'll order new ones.

We played chess in the evening with the "travel" chess set I brought from home. I'm getting better, I win once in a while. Life here is simple, quiet, and peaceful.

I wonder how many visitors were introduced to Jesus for the first time today.

Friday, September 22, 2023

Mark 3:7-19

Whenever the unclean spirits saw Him, they would fall down before Him and shout, "You are the Son of God."

Mark 3:11

Even the evil spirits of that day recognized Jesus. But knowing His identity is not enough, is it? There must be submission to His authority and sovereignty. I never want to water down the Gospel and lead people to think they have a seat at the Heavenly table when, in fact, they do not. The Holy Spirit points to Jesus as the Messiah in order for one to genuinely receive Him as Savior and Lord.

FOUND! The badge and keys fell out of the chair cushions this morning. How can it be that I missed that during the deep clean search? The find caused a friendly "celebration" during devotions.

This morning, we took a walk in the nearby Muslim area and discovered two English bookstores! What a delight! Children's books are very prominent. There must be an English-speaking community close by.

This afternoon, we watched on my phone the online stream of the wedding of the daughter of a favorite Garden Tomb couple who live in Jerusalem but were originally from the Netherlands. The parents of the bride are sweet, godly people who serve their community well, and we love them. Weddings here are very different than those we've attended in Dallas, to say the least. There is a great emphasis put on the family members who bless the newlyweds, give advice, and promise support. These conversations take place during the ceremony itself, with each family group approaching the altar for encouraging conversations. The joy of the young couple and their parents and friends is the same as we might experience in the US, even though the ceremony itself lasted two hours. What a privilege to be invited to watch this event.

We spent the evening at an apartment of staff people with other American friends, laughing, chatting, and comparing notes from our day.

These four-hour shifts are terrific. The exhaustion I feared and have experienced on past trips is no more. All the volunteers love it, perhaps because most of us are old and our bodies just aren't cooperating like they did at one time. The volunteer staff are usually older folks that have the time to pack up and move to a foreign country, whereas young folks are still working or going to school to begin their careers.

Saturday, September 23, 2023

Mark 3:20-30

"If a house is divided against itself, that house will not be able *to stand.*"
Mark 3:25

The nation of Israel is so divided with thick almost visible tension throughout. Jerusalem has been conquered time and time again and yet it stands as God's chosen city. Religious differences are blatantly obvious and proclaimed throughout. The scriptures tell us that one day the King of Kings will reign from this place and all differences will be resolved as every knee shall bow. When, Lord Jesus?

Can the worship time during morning devotions get any better? Our director's wife played the guitar, and a gifted staff member played the keyboard. The singing is simply wonderful. What a great start to our day! We hear the word each morning, pray in stunned silence, pray aloud together, and sing enthusiastically. The unity and peace are strong.

This morning, I cleaned the fridge! Household chores do not go away, even in this incredible place.

I served as prayer guide again this afternoon and watched as an elderly man fainted at the approach to the tomb. The ambulance came and took him to the hospital. It was an upsetting event, but everyone helped.

Later in the day, I was surprised to reunite with a young woman from Hungary that we'd met and served with at the Garden a few years ago. We had a long talk, she's moving to Jerusalem permanently and has a job with a Christian organization. It was a wonderful visit and we made plans to meet for dinner later in the month. It's true, everyone comes to Jerusalem sometime in their life!

At 6 p.m., we all gathered at the gate for a quick walk to the Azarrah Hotel, our favorite dining place for the whole group.

Twenty-five of us paraded through the dark streets of the Muslim section of East Jerusalem. Muslim men line the sidewalks and shops, motorcycles whizz by us, and car horns seem pretty constant in this neighborhood. The streets seemed cleaner this time, and we wondered why the people in this part of the West Bank decided to pick up trash and sweep their sidewalks. The hotel is in a typical Middle Eastern style, and the restaurant offers Muslim cuisine. The pizza is a favorite, but the "ham" looks an awful lot like our American boloney! The bi-monthly fellowship is terrific, and the Garden picks up the bill as a treat and appreciation for all the hard work done by the volunteers. We work, play, pray, and eat together with joy. We live in a community.

Sunday, September 24, 2023
No staff devotions today.

After a few days of cooler weather, we had to turn the AC back on. Thankfully, all the apartments have A/C. We had lunch today at Notre Dame's beautiful buffet dining room. We had no idea this facility was open to the public. What a treat! We plan to return to this lovely place many times in the next few weeks.

We texted Andy's contact at the Church of the Holy Sepulcher and made an appointment for a private tour on Tuesday at 2 p.m.

We received our schedule for next week, we'll have 3 ½ days off work. That will give us time to explore the newer parts of Jerusalem.

We ended the afternoon playing chess outside on the upstairs patio right outside our door.

We can hear the Muslim family next door playing. Thankfully, they don't have a dog!! We've heard too many stories of dogs being tied up, ignored, and barking continuously.

Monday, September 25, 2023
Mark 3:21-25

"Truly, I say to you, all sins shall be forgiven the sons of men."
Mark 3:28

What an offer from the Savior! What a life-changing event! How often do I share this news?

YOM KIPPUR! This morning, our devotion time was spent at Skull Hill. A wooden cross was laid on the ground as Simon, our director, led us with thoughts of atonement. This day is the Jewish highest holy day of the year, when the day is spent in repentance, asking for forgiveness for all the sins of the past year. The slate is wiped clean! Since there is no longer a blood sacrifice because there is no Jewish temple, everyone stays home in private worship.

The Jewish parts of the city are closed. There are no cars, no people, and no sound! Only children on bicycles are out, and they are racing down the main highways with no fear of traffic. There is a heavy military and police presence everywhere. If a conflict occurs between Muslims and Jews, it usually happens on a significant Jewish holy day. There are barricades up in the streets to keep vehicles away from the Jewish sections.

We walked up to Jaffe Gate and were stunned by the lack of life as far as the eye could see. Jewish shops, restaurants, and the Manilla Mall were quiet. It's a day of prayer.

In the afternoon, we took a nap and studied the history of the city.

We texted Granddaughter Gracie at 4 am. Our family and friends have no idea how we miss them.

Have our Jewish neighbors received forgiveness on this day? Oh, that they would be drawn to the Messiah.

Tuesday, September 26, 2023

Mark 4:1-20

"To you have been given the mysteries of the kingdom of God."

Mark 4:11

God, in His goodness and mercy, does not stay hidden. His characteristics can be known through the scriptures. People ask me, "How can I know God?" The answers lie in their open Bible. Thank you, Lord, for not hiding Yourself or Your plans from us.

We took our US volunteer friend to the Jewish Market and the IWO Butcher Shop today. Oh, my, that was so much fun. He is delighted to know of this special place and stocked up his refrigerator too.

At 2 p.m., we met with the Assistant to the "Holy Beatitude". He is the high priest of the Armenian sector of the church. His assistant is such a vibrant young woman, and she gave us a behind-the-scenes tour of the Church of the Holy Sepulcher. All at once, bells started ringing, and everyone around us started getting really excited. Evidently, something big was about to happen. Our new friend explained that a parade of priests was about to begin to celebrate the day the cross of Jesus was discovered. We lined up and waited. She hid behind us so her "boss" wouldn't see her because she was not wearing a dress! The bells rang out, and soon a gaggle of priests came around the corner outside the door of the church, and the march started. Two men on either side of the "Holy Beatitude" held long sticks that they pounded on the ground in marching time. About twenty black-robed, long white-bearded, tall-hatted priests followed their leader into the church. Tourists and locals lined the pathway. That was impressive.

We climbed the tiny staircase to the top of the church, where small huts/buildings housed the Ethiopian priests. Oh, my! Then we traveled downward to the huge Cistern of St. Helen below. There is so much history in this place. Our new friend/guide explained that Israel is now trying to stop worship services inside the church, claiming the building is a fire hazard and dangerous. She is very upset at the prospect of church services being banned after thousands of years of worship there. She is angry at Israel, claiming they are trying to suppress Christian work and worship in Jerusalem.

That's a lot to ponder in this very complex environment.

Wednesday, September 27, 2023
Mark 4:21-25

"A lamp is not brought to be put under a basket, is it, or under a bed?"

Mark 4:21

What good is the light that is hidden? Our relationship with Jesus is personal, but must not be private. He is to be proclaimed always.

The devotion this morning was all about light. Our wise director urged us to "go and light the darkness."

The light of the gospel is critical in this world of darkness. It's evident on the bright, shiny faces of His people who come through the gate each day. Those who know the power of the gospel to bring forgiveness, peace, and restoration are eager to come to this place. I am very aware of the contrast that I see on the faces of the Muslim women who walk beside me on the streets. They are sad, and their eyes have no light. I can only imagine what goes on in their homes on a daily basis. They are like "ghosts" roaming about, having no voice or even an acknowledgement that they exist. Most women in the United States that I know have no idea of the incredible privileges they have by simply being born in America.

Dennis guided groups this afternoon, and I served as a prayer guide.

Sharing the gospel many times every day is a joy unmatched. Praying with people is such a privilege, as they realize someone cares for them and wants to spend time with them. So many people who come through the gate are bearing some type of burden; sometimes they share their pain, and we pray together.

This evening, the staff member in charge of training volunteers gave us a review as we visited each important site in the garden. We noticed an Israeli drone flying about our heads which was a little odd, but we waved at whoever was monitoring that thing. The garden is simply beautiful now; the trees and flowers are lush, and the grapes growing in the arched arbor at the entrance are turning purple. That is so lovely and reminds everyone that this area was once a vineyard. It was an easy day.

We have a dear friend in America who is right now attending her brother's funeral and grieving with the rest of the family. It's hard to be on the other side of the world when friends back home are hurting. We are separated by distance, but our thoughts and prayers are with them.

Thursday, September 28, 2023

Mark 4:26-34

"The kingdom of God is like a man who casts seed upon the soil,"

Mark 4:26

So many different types of people, so many difference types of spiritual "soil" come through the gate. It seems we are casting seeds of the knowledge of God sometimes and then we leave the growth of that seed up to others that come along to encourage, train, and nurture. I pray everyone that hears the Gospel for the first time will become involved in a local church to receive follow up love, guidance and community support.

The Directors are visiting Galilee today to discuss a garden that is planned to be built there. That will be exciting. They will certainly be good advisors for that project.

The dear retired pastor from England presented the staff devotion this morning; it was excellent. What wonderful people the Lord has brought to this place. He has great insight, and his love for the Lord is so very evident.

There's a virus going around, and one then another is coming down with tummy trouble. A few volunteers have contracted COVID, and they are isolated for days. It's amazing that we don't have more plagues with the number of people we are seeing coming through the gate from all different countries. I make and take my famous chicken soup to the sick and afflicted. It's sure to cure any ailment. (I'm always on the search for celery for my soup!)

I prepared communion for the visitors this morning, Dennis guided several groups. My apple watch says I walked 5, 485 steps by 4:15, and the day is young.

The permanent staff are all off today, and it seems a little chaotic.

We "scrounged" for food again at the Muslim market nearby. It was its usual fiasco.

Tonight, several of us walked through the Damascus Gate into the Old City at the invitation of a previous Dallas citizen who lives right on the Via Delarosa. She is an old friend of our Dallas volunteer and originally lived in Dallas, having graduated from Southern Methodist University. What a delightful story and an absolutely beautiful home right on the Via Delarosa. She shared her struggles with marriages, deaths, buying property in the Old City, and living day to day in a Muslim community. Her Christian heart loves every stone in Jerusalem. We were very honored to be guests in her beautiful home. Her father visited the Garden Tomb years ago, and she shared pictures of that visit. We look forward to seeing her again in Jerusalem and Dallas.

Friday, September 29, 2023

Mark 4:35-41

"Why are you afraid? Do you still have no faith?"
Mark 4:40

Evidently, Jesus connected fear to faith. His words! And I'm reminded of Romans 8:38 "For I am convinced that neither death, nor life, nor angels, nor principalities, nor things present, nor things to come, nor powers, nor height, nor depth, nor any other created thing, will be able to separate us from the love of God, which is in Christ Jesus our Lord." That's pretty secure.

I spent all morning studying which is very easy here, there are no distractions. We have no TV or radio, but get a few glimpses of news on Dennis's computer once in a while. We are pretty isolated from world news. It's easy to imagine a peaceful world as we enjoy the peace in our little apartment on a quiet morning.

I prepared communion again this afternoon. After delivering the elements to the worship sites I continually walk through the Garden to pick up empty communion trays after groups have left. Washing them and storing for the next group is busy work but a quiet alone time in the kitchen.

So many miles are racked up on my comfy orthopedic sandals. Brief rests and visits with other volunteer guides, waiting for their assignment to groups, and sitting outside the kitchen door are delightful times. All kinds of problems are solved, jokes are told, recipes are shared, stories are recounted, scriptures are read, and history is reviewed during those waiting times. I teasingly call that spot of plastic outdoor chairs the gathering of the "Sanhedrin."

Tour groups arrived all afternoon, with a huge group from the US. One man lost his passport, and that created a buzz. His group leader and the GT staff kicked into action, but it looked pretty hopeless since this was Friday, Shabbat, and no official US offices would be open until Monday morning. The tour group's plane was to leave within hours. We never heard what happened in that situation. Perhaps the man and his immediate family stayed in Israel until the US embassy could help him. Hopefully, the people at the embassy came through for him.

That blue passport is critical in this country. It is the ticket to anywhere you want to go, places that Israelis and Palestinians are barred from entering. Preferential treatment is given to those who carry it. We are always stunned at the freedom it gives us, the freedom that people who live in the land do not have.

Today marked the beginning of Sukkot, the Feast of
Tabernacles. Makeshift huts are appearing all over the city in the Jewish neighborhoods. Some are very modest plastic and plywood, while in the wealthier sections of the city, they are very elaborate tents made of canvas, draperies, flowers, and food. Jewish families live in those huts, celebrating the time when God lived with them in the Tabernacle in the wilderness. Christians celebrate the feast by reminding each other when the Lord will once again physically walk among us. It is a festive time. Thousands of Jews from all over the world come to Israel for this holiday season. Christians come to join the festivities and celebrate with their Jewish friends. The city is full of people. The light rail is packed and dangerously full. Orthodox Jewish men are scurrying about carrying palm branches and lemons wrapped in cellophane that must be used in ceremonies. Many find their way to the Western Wall for a priestly blessing. Thousands and thousands of people fill the Western Wall Plaza almost nightly.

We walked down to the Wall about 6 p.m. to see a priestly blessing but it was rescheduled. We heard later that the crowd appeared at 1 a.m. and the blessing was given then. We wondered if the timing of these blessings are to prevent "outsiders" from coming to watch.

I am often approached by a Jewish man of authority to stop taking pictures down at the Wall. They are very protective of the activities there.

Saturday, September 30, 2023

Mark 5:1-20

"Come out of the man, you unclean spirit."

Mark 5:8

As much as I'd like to ignore this verse, I have to come to grips with the fact that there are "unclean spirits" in our world and in some people. Compassion leads me to make excuses for some people's behavior when, in fact, demons are real and cause havoc and evil deeds. BUT, Jesus has authority over them as well. What a Savior! I bring those suffering to Him through prayer.

After morning devotions and much prayer, I did laundry again. Our guide uniform is dark pants and a red polo shirt, so we can be identified by visitors. It's a great plan, but living in this desert heat involves regular laundry. I learned after our first visit here that bringing cute clothes and shoes from Dallas is a waste of effort, time, and weight! I've skinned down my packing list to the bare essentials, and it's a great fashion lifestyle. A few cool nondescript items to wear into the city to explore on days off, a straw hat and comfy shoes are all that's needed. Long sleeves and high necklines are required, and a big scarf to cover anything else is my advice for future pilgrims. Otherwise, you'll be questioned by the Muslim fashion police on the Temple Mount.

And it's always best to be respectful of cultures when you're a foreign visitor.

During the afternoon shift I served as gatekeeper and counted 400 people "walking-in" without a reservation, tour guide or group. We are seeing an increase in that category of visitors. Each one received a greeting, information and often a personal visit from a prayer guide. People from all nations walked through that gate. It's a busy task and you never know who is about to enter through that green iron door. Some are thrilled to be here, others perplexed and confused, but all are welcome.

Dennis guided many groups around the site this afternoon. He grins from ear to ear, and the people love him. Sometimes, they look for him after their worship service to give him a blessing.

There was a huge fiasco with a group of tourists today. It involved a terrible confrontation with them at the tomb entrance. Some cultures are difficult and a challenge to guide as they demand doing things their way, regardless of how their actions cause chaos for others. The newly appointed operations manager experienced his "trial by fire." The director closed the shop so that the group could not enter and then escorted them out of the front gate. It's very upsetting to think that some people so misbehave that they are barred from returning to this very peaceful place. Sometimes it's a cultural problem, but mostly it's just people running amok or perhaps "unclean spirits" showing themselves. Everyone is treated with dignity, no matter how they behave. We pray every day that we will always love as Jesus loved.

Sunday, October 1, 2023
No staff devotions today.

We slept in and skipped church at Christ's Church this morning. The city is so very crowded and the pastor is out of the country. We used both as an excuse to rest.

We took the light rail to Ben Yehuda for shopping and lunch. This street is lined with shops, restaurants, street musicians and food smells. Huge crowds are everywhere, excitement is in the air. Families are celebrating Sukkot and a festive atmosphere permeates every alley, restaurant, balcony and home. It's fun to watch the Jewish families herding their children into restaurants. Darling children are playing in the streets. We got back to the apartment at about 1 p.m.

At 3:30 p.m., we met with 10 other volunteers at the gate to go to the King David Hotel to celebrate a volunteer's birthday together. We waited at the train stop for a long time, and a soldier finally told us that there was a bomb threat at the previous stop, so the train would be delayed for a while. That was the first time we'd experienced news of a bomb. We decided to WALK! Oh, my.

We walked 30 minutes uphill and downhill, and just as we were about to approach this fabulous, historic hotel, the train went whizzing by. Wouldn't you know it?

The King David Hotel is THE place for dignitaries, presidents, prime ministers, and all the powerful people to stay. It is stately, grand, and beautiful. We were escorted out to the patio where we enjoyed tea and desserts while overlooking the beautiful grounds, pool, trees, and lovely people. Touring the hotel itself was a treat. We shared tea and treats with the group, sang to the birthday girl, and had a lovely afternoon in that magnificent place.

We walked that long way back to the Garden, where the director showed us the new glass installed at the tomb entrance and viewing platform above. His job of overseeing the contractors and workers must be very stressful at times, but he handles each situation with authority and grace. Deadlines and timelines are pushed here, too.

We're wondering how anything gets done in this city. Workers again brought mattresses and clothing and stayed overnight in the Emmaus Chapel in order to be able to start work early every morning. The glass walkway at the entrance to the tomb is beautiful. The awkward steps getting into the tomb are gone, yet the ground below is still visible. The whole project is designed to make the entrance easier and smoother for large groups that will be arriving in October and November. So many preparations are being made to accommodate the largest number of tourists who have made advance reservations and will soon be returning to the land since before the COVID pandemic.

A very generous donor from Texas gave half a million dollars to pay for the project. Her gift was unsolicited and came as a huge surprise. The "Friends of the Garden, USA" foundation funneled that gift to Israel. Dennis was so very excited to share that news since he's serving on that board. Everyone was so very grateful; the board of the GT Association was stunned, and much praise was given to the Lord for meeting this need in His own very creative way. God's hand has always been on this ministry. HE never fails to provide.

My Apple Watch says I walked 5.94 miles today, 15,626 steps. A record!

Monday, October 2, 2023
Mark 5:21-34

"If I just touch His garments, I will be well."
Mark 5:28

The power of faith in Jesus brings change. I'm reminded that it is not the size of my faith that moves mountains, but the size of the object of my faith. Jesus has proven Himself time and time again as the Son of God, Creator, and Sustainer of all life. I can bring all my problems to Him and He will handle them in His way and in His time.

A huge impressive international organization showed up today and we had 2000 visitors enjoying worship this morning. They are in Jerusalem for the Jewish holidays, The ICJM organization that comes every year. They had very interesting personal translation devices for many languages set up for the people to use. What a fantastic and very busy time. The air was full of beautiful singing, preaching and even dancing at times.

Some women dance to lovely music while twirling long colorful ribbons. Others are dressed in their native costumes while so many simply enjoy worshipping freely since they are forbidden to do so in their home country. There are many tears of gratitude.

We are always amazed and accepting of the variety of worship styles that must please the Heavenly Father. The American church culture shows up when the Texans arrive, and that is so much fun and familiar.

We both guided groups in the afternoon, telling the story of Jesus again and again. Even believers returning year after year to this sacred place are always encouraged.

Tuesday, October 3, 2023

Mark 5:35-43

"Do not be afraid any longer, only believe."

Mark 5:36

It seems that the scripture says belief in the Lord Jesus is the path to courage. Here in this place we believe that God is Sovereign over all of us, our families, this nation and the world. He is not surprised by anything and is involved in the details of all our lives. The Bible tells me so. What have I to fear? He has redeemed my soul; everything else is minor!

We had the whole day off, which started with a farmer's style breakfast of eggs, bacon, and all the trimmings at a neighboring volunteer's apartment. What a lovely fellowship is possible when everyone agrees that the gospel of Jesus Christ is the focus of living. We live in a bubble of God's grace.

After a trip to the Jewish "Skuk," the famous outdoor market, we packed into the light rail cars with thousands of other men, women, and children of all shapes, sizes, and nationalities. One Jewish mother insisted upon pushing her baby stroller onto the train car after the door closed on her several times. I watched, concerned that the baby was going to be cut into two pieces! She somehow squeezed that thing in. We were all packed like sardines in a tin can. It was a terrible ordeal. Too many folks in Jerusalem! The Holidays bring people to Jerusalem from all over the world. Excitement is in the air!

I wonder how many of these thousands of locals and visitors are truly celebrating the King of Kings or the elements of their culture.

Wednesday, October 4, 2023

Mark 6:1-6

"A prophet is not without honor except in His own hometown and among his own relatives and in his own household."

Mark 6:4

Jesus, the Son of God, the One that performed miracles right before their very eyes was not honored as Deity in His hometown. The locals knew Him as the son of Mary, they knew His earthly dad, where He lived, and how He spent His time. He was the illegitimate child living down the way. They couldn't see past their own ideas of just who He was. Familiarity sometimes blinds the ones who know Him. Today I want to see the wonder of Jesus afresh.

Laundry again this morning. It's a clear, sunny day, which is the best day for hanging our laundry outside on the patio. It dries in no time! So much time and energy is spent on mundane but very necessary chores. I developed a new appreciation for my gas dryer in Texas. We Americans are very spoiled!

Tonight, we joined other volunteers on a special tour. Twelve of us embarked on a walking tour of Mia Sharim, the ultra-orthodox neighborhood that is nearby. We were warned not to take pictures, to walk as if on a mission, to dress very modestly, and not to stop or make a spectacle of ourselves. It has been proven that these folks do not like Christians, but no violence has been reported lately.

We were told years ago on our first trip to Jerusalem that if a tour bus or a car drove down those crowded streets during Shabbat, they would be stoned. We were taking no chances of that.

The area is like visiting another world. The streets are dark and dirty, and the people have many, many smiling, happy children, but they live in extremely poor conditions. The men spend their time studying the Torah, day after day, exempt from serving in the Israeli military, even though all other Israeli young men and women are required to serve 2 years. The very young soldiers are always in the city laughing, talking, and eating while balancing their personal AK-47 on their shoulders. They are obviously missing in the neighborhood of Mia Sharim.

After walking a good distance, we found the 24-hour. The bakery everyone brags about. What an amazing place! All kinds of bread, treats, and sweets were lined up on huge shelved carts, with more coming out of the ovens all the time. That wonderful, freshly baked bread smell is intoxicating. We all indulged and bought way too many sweets. It takes a lot of bread and cakes to feed all those people. No wonder this bakery is in operation all day, every day!

The dark back alleys were lined with the small, make shift huts made from plywood and plastic, which served as their dwelling places during Sukkot. I kept watching for rats, but there seemed to be a good supply of hungry cats. The experience was surreal.

There is a spiritual darkness here.

We walked back to the GT and fell into bed exhausted.

Thursday, October 5, 2023

Mark 6:7-16

"They went out and preached that men should repent."

Mark 6:12

Who wants to hear that a change is needed in their life? Pride gets in the way of true repentance. Only the Holy Spirit can convict of wrong doing but the disciples were commanded to speak the word repent. Is it an act of love to tell people the truth?

The weather has cooled off and the A/C is shut off. It's good to open all the windows and the front door of the apartment, which allows sounds from the city and close neighbors to filter in. We live in such tight quarters with the other volunteers, it's truly a family situation. Smelling what the neighbor is cooking or listening to the Jewish children is playing nearby accentuates the closeness, but there's a sense of peace and calm.

I finished my study for the upcoming Mark presentation and emailed my notes to the staff member in charge of all things computer-related. He printed them and delivered them promptly. He's so very good and highly respected. And did I say, legally blind? What a wonderful friend and co-worker in the kingdom. He is a favorite guide and leads people with his white cane tapping on the stone pavements.

Dennis guided in the afternoon, and I again served as gatekeeper. Many lovely people entered, and some loud, very manipulative Israeli guides entered. We enjoyed the differences in culture and made friends with all who came in. We deal with all kinds of personalities, too, and if any controversy arises, we are to contact the receptionist, who handles situations very quickly and gracefully.

We see a cross section of humanity here every day and when confronted with the truth of the Gospel very often tears of repentance often flow. Lives are changed.

Friday, October 6, 2023

Mark 6:17-29

"When the disciples heard about this, they came and took away his body and laid it in a tomb."

Mark 6:29

The body of Jesus was preserved with spices and wrapped in linen and laid in a tomb. There was such respect for His physical body. It was not burned on a pier, cast into water or desecrated in any way. I wonder if this burial was to be an example or, as some would say, just a cultural event.

We just received several pictures of the great grandson Brooks today. He now has 4 teeth and smiles and laughs a lot. Hays, our grandson, is thrilled that his son's little personality is developing and that he is now no longer just a "lump."

At devotion time today, we learned that one of our dear volunteers from Indiana suffered a heart attack last night. He was taken to the hospital by the director and transferred to another hospital for treatment. Our resident nurse believes he would have a stent procedure. We prayed fervently for his recovery.

We walked through the Jaffe Gate to the Christian Quarter in search of a shop recommended by the Dallas transplant who lives on the Via Delarosa. We were to look for a guy named Phu-Wad, who could be found in a shop with a big arched entrance, perhaps the Oriental Bazaar.

After asking for directions from several locals and wondering through stone alleys, we stumbled upon the shop, looking for Phu-Wad. The man in front of us stated that yes, he was Phu Wad! We purchased a beautiful blue tablecloth and a table runner there, and four Jerusalem crosses from a shop across the alley. Part of this experience is shopping for treasures, but we have to be very careful and buy from recommended shops. Shysters are everywhere, even in the Holy City.

Back at the Garden Tomb, we shared communion with the staff and volunteers. The worship times we have together are priceless and my favorite part of this experience. Meeting several times a day with them is fine with me. The whole atmosphere of this place reeks of peace. All is well here, all are focused on the beauty and peace of Jesus.

All these wonderful things are happening in a cemetery. Tombs surround the area especially in the compound of St. Stephens Basilica right next door, and the Muslim cometary which is located above Skull Hill and the wall of the Garden Tomb.

Life is lived, and new life is offered in the place of the dead.

PART II
WAR
SUPERNATURAL PEACE
October 7, 2023
Mark 6:30-44

"Come away by yourselves to a secluded place and rest a while."
Mark 6:31

There are so many delightful visitors, singing, praying, walking, and taking communion, it's so easy to get caught up in the "work" we do and sometimes lose our focus on the One we do it for, the One we adore. Making time to be alone with the Lord is a top priority. Strength, peace, purpose, joy, and delight come from Him alone.

I woke up celebrating the fact that I had no foot pain and was delighted that today I would be serving as a prayer guide again. That position is becoming my favorite thing to do. It's always a one-on-one conversation with a tourist after my one-on-one conversation with the Father!

We had just finished a great time of singing and reading the scripture together in the staff room when the AIR RAID SIREN blasted throughout the area. For a few brief moments, all were stunned. None of us had ever heard that siren before. Never. I remember praying aloud, "Lord, something terrible is happening right now, please be very near those who are in harm's way, protect us here." Our circumstantial peace was shattered.

The director proclaimed, "Go to the bomb shelter, you have 90 seconds before there will be an explosion." We all left together very quickly and quietly. We raced down the stairs to the outside, across the ancient pathways, and down more marble stones to the Emmaus Chapel. It is underground, newly renovated, and serves as a bomb shelter. We sat on the benches together in stunned silence. We heard the bombs exploding overhead as the missiles fired were intercepted by the Israel Defense system called the Iron Dome.

We were told that the Emmaus Chapel and the Large Chapel near Skull Hill were the designated bomb shelters and that anytime we heard the siren, we should make our way to the closest one. If caught outdoors, further away from those places, we are to lie flat on the ground to make a smaller target of ourselves in order to prevent bodily damage by shrapnel from an explosion.

After about 10 minutes, we were given the "all clear" sign, and as we left the Emmaus Chapel, we could see the contrails overhead because the missiles aimed at Jerusalem were destroyed.

Surely, this was a one-off situation, but the director and permanent staff quickly contacted the military and local officials. The reality was conveyed: **Israel had declared war on Gaza.**

We knew no more details.

And it was time to open the gate for the tourists that had lined up in the alley approaching the entrance.

Several groups entered and the siren started wailing again. I joined several tourists in the Emmaus Chapel. Other guides were lying on the ground with their tourists, all in a state of shock. The children were confused and frightened.

One young lady was sitting alone, wide-eyed and frightened. I sat beside her and learned her name was Pam, from Ohio, touring Israel by herself. I hugged her and quietly informed her that war had been declared, and she must find a way to get out of the country as soon as possible. She started shaking, and I held her and talked quietly until we were both smiling and resting in the sovereignty of God, confident that HE was not surprised by these events and would lead us all to safety. We prayed for all involved. After the "all clear," she wandered in the Garden a bit, and another siren sounded, and we found ourselves together again.

This time, she was confident that she would be alright and was making plans to leave. We said goodbye with smiles and well wishes. I wondered if I'd ever see my new friend again. I'm sorry that I forgot to ask her for her last name.

The decision was made to evacuate the Garden and send the tourists back to their hotels, where they could "shelter in place" safely. A Chinese group refused to leave. After much conversation, they conveyed their concern for us! They didn't want to leave the staff and volunteers, they wanted to stay with us and pray.

A temporary silence settled in, and we were told to "shelter in place." That meant we were to go back to our apartments, pray, wait, and try to stay busy there.

The quiet was deafening, and we decided to clean the apartment just to be busy and take our minds off the reality that was happening outside our gate. I remember telling Dennis, "We are going to die here, let's pray for a quick death and no lingering under concrete for days on end." And, "we might as well have a clean apartment if we're going to be bombed." We worked feverishly just to keep our minds and bodies busy.

Soon, we could hear the sounds of heavy military planes and helicopters flying overhead. How could anything of such magnitude be happening when we felt so safe in our little apartment?

Gunfire started in the streets nearby. More sirens, more contrails in the sky. More trips to the bomb shelter.

After one period of calm, the director decided to open the gate once again, stating, "We have what people need, a place of peace and the news of the gospel." A few people trickled in, and a few groups of tourists found themselves stranded in the city with no place to go.

We soon learned that all international airlines suspended flights in and out of Ben Gurion Airport in Tel Aviv. There was no way out of the country, yet there was no fear in our hearts. Circumstantial peace had been replaced by the Supernatural peace of God. Only HIS peace can explain the lack of panic, fear, tears, or anxiety.

We are praying without ceasing for so many caught up in this terrible situation.

We collapsed in bed.

Sunday, October 8, 2023
We missed staff devotions this morning.

No personal devotions this morning. My mind is filled.

I woke up at 2 a.m., answering texts and emails. Family and friends in the States were clamoring for news. They are frightened by pictures on their TVs about events that they knew nothing about. "We are safe and unafraid" is our message to the kids, Illinois family, and Dallas friends. Our daughter-in-law and grandchildren are praying and texting. Friends from Little Rock and Savannah are worried. After two hours of communicating, I finally went back to sleep.

Large, heavy airplane engines roared overhead.

The news is horrific; there was an attack on an Israeli Kibbutz near Gaza and a musical festival near the Gaza border on Saturday, which left thousands dead and many kidnapped. This "skirmish" is different than any other we've experienced or heard about.

All flights in and out of Israel are still cancelled until further notice.

Sons Andy and Philip are concerned and texting. There is a plan being discussed for our "immediate extraction," and we are to make a decision on Monday. Philip wants to charter a plane to "come get us." As good as that sounds, no planes are permitted to land.

The day was eerily quiet, there were no bus engines or horns, no planes overhead, no military jets, rockets, or sirens.

Hamas is firing rockets from the south, and Hezbollah fires rockets from the north, from Lebanon. We heard that the Taliban wanted to enter and join the fight. Dennis says, "Israel will put a rocket up their tailpipe." We are not sure what to believe.

We arranged for the news to be broadcast on his laptop, and it's blaring constantly.

The Garden is always closed on Sunday, so it's empty as usual.

We walked up to Skull Hill and saw two buses returning to the Muslim bus stop below, and only two people walking on the street. No new passengers, all the buses are parked in the very full lot, a scene we'd never witnessed before. Everyone is in hiding.

Two of our UK friends wanted to leave immediately, and we, too, began to search for flights to anywhere in Europe. A ticket on Virgin Airlines to London on Friday is a possibility.

The director called a meeting for noon in the staff room, and all attended. He assured us that the choice to leave now or stay was completely our decision, that there would be no judgement, nor would our decision affect any future invitation to return. The atmosphere was one of seriousness, but great praise to the Lord. God's supernatural peace settled in over the staff and volunteers.

News of the atrocities committed by Hamas near the Gaza border trickled into the Garden. So many rapes, murders and kidnappings. Over 250 hostages were taken from their homes, children were killed in front of their parents, babies were beheaded, soldiers were tortured and captured, babies were burned alive in ovens, and over 1200 Jews were slaughtered. How can this be possible? How can the rage against the Jews rise again to this level of evil? Has the world learned nothing from history? Shock and sadness have replaced the joy we'd been experiencing.

The family insisted that we register with the American Embassy.
We filled out the forms, and they assured us they would "contact us."

The afternoon wore on and we "zoomed" our Sunday School Class back in Frisco. That gave us a sense of normalcy and we assured them we were "safe and unafraid."

Monday, October 9, 2023

Mark 6:45-56

"Take courage, it is I, do not be afraid."

Mark 6:50

**HE has promised to be with us, even to the end of the age.
Neither life nor death will separate us from the love of God. How do people survive this life without Jesus? No matter the situations we face, we are confident that God is sovereign and He is surprised by nothing. We are not afraid.**

Devotions were very somber this morning. Two of our staff members are young women who live in the West Bank and arrived late with very worried looks on their faces, both near tears.

They are experiencing life very differently from the rest of us. They are not "safe and unafraid" in their own homes and are concerned for their families and friends. They know some of the young people who were kidnapped and killed by Hamas.

We sang praises to our God, and a theme is developing. Jesus has become our Hiding Place.

Our hearts are encouraged.

No matter what might come, we feel safe in His loving hands. Neither the atrocities of life nor the certainty of death will shake us. We feel physically and spiritually safe in this lovely Garden with these godly friends. Everyone here is dependent on the Lord, and all are very aware of His presence.

The morning was quiet and as Dennis searched the internet, he asked if I wanted to go to Paris, Dubai, or Turkey. He booked a flight to Paris on Air France, we could stay a week and catch our original United Flight back to the US as originally planned. It sounds so simple.

Oh my, I would love to spend a week in Paris! Friends and family are praying that this flight will happen. Two other volunteers have flights that same day, perhaps we can ride to the airport together. It's going to happen.

I planned menus for the week. Life had to go on while we waited.

The sirens started wailing again at noon. We all headed for the bomb shelter; there were several groups from Brazil already there when I arrived. A lovely staff member started singing. Singing calmed everyone's nerves. Men and women were kneeling by the benches, some were crying.

One woman loudly declared that she was a pastor and started yelling scriptures about not being afraid. Her voice echoed in the shelter, frightening everyone. Our local Israeli staff member got everyone's attention and told her to be quiet so we could hear the "all clear" sound. Things quieted immediately, but several Brazilian women were still very frightened and crying softly. Such an unusual scene for this place.

The all-clear sounded, and everyone left the shelter. The afternoon progressed, and I led a lovely group of Germans at 4 p.m. What very sweet people. They hung on to every word of the gospel. Many felt we all might be seeing the Lord personally very soon. There is a remarkable calmness, but that's what the gospel provides, isn't it?

Andy face timed us this evening. He's keeping up with friends in East Jerusalem and the political scene. The airlines are still suspending flights.

The volunteer who had the heart attack has returned to his apartment here in the Garden. He seemed very weak but was still praising God. It is so good to have him back in the Garden where he is loved and cared for. His doctor said that he cannot fly for 3-4 weeks. He and his wife will be the last to leave if and when flights resume.

We are not afraid. He is with us, and He is with our dear friend, too.

Tuesday, October 10, 2023

Mark 7:1-13

"The people honor Me with their lips but their heart is far away from Me."

Mark 7:6b

Only God sees the heart. Only He knows if a person genuinely loves Him or if one is just speaking words of praise. What is Jesus seeing when He looks at my heart? Does obedience characterize my life?

A lovely volunteer from the UK led devotions this morning. She stressed the command to "fear not." What a righteous time of singing and praising God. Surely the Lord is in this place.

The director announced that the new hours for opening the Garden would now be 9-4. That schedule is subject to change daily.

The teasing continues, as one volunteer teases another that they've arranged for him to leave immediately, but he must "leave his bacon behind." The forbidden bacon is always the subject of ongoing smiles because the smell of pork cooking permeates the whole area often.

About mid-morning, we were aware of a new "crisis." The staff room was out of their normal cookies and milk. We were asked if we would walk to the local shop to purchase these necessities of life, the owner would know "which kind we normally buy," and we were to put it on the Garden Tomb account. We raced out of the gate, having a fun moment in an otherwise surreal situation. We watched carefully for anyone who might come close to us who could possibly be a terrorist, but the streets were almost empty. We were not to draw attention to ourselves, and did not speak because our accent would reveal that we are American. I wondered how our American appearance could be hidden! We were off on a high adventure, a memory in the making. We laughed about how willing we were to lay down our lives for cookies!

The cookies and milk were purchased after much discussion with the owner of the shop (who speaks only broken English), and we raced back to the safety of the Garden compound! Mission accomplished. There was a lot of laughter at the Gate once everyone realized we'd successfully purchased the correct items in the middle of a war zone! There's joy in the little things! Evidently, cookies are a priority even as rockets are being fired overhead.

A thunderstorm moved in about 3 p.m. Rain, glorious rain in this desert land.

While chatting with other volunteers our Palestinian friend that serves in the gift shop, shared the customs of Muslim marriages. Oh yes, everything is discussed when you live so close together and now have a lot of time to talk.

We learned that Palestinian customs demand a dowry that Muslim men must pay to the family of the bride. A lot of gold is presented to the bride and her family. The purpose is to provide for the bride should the marriage not work out! Oh, my. Learning the traditions of other cultures is an added benefit of living in a foreign country. This beautiful Palestinian Christian friend was always a source of joy and praise to the Lord. No one sings like this gal. We love her dearly. Palestinian Christians are the folks low on the totem pole in Israel. They are most often dismissed as "invisible people' but not here in the Garden. Everyone is treated with respect and dignity.

The Muslim call to pray continues 5 times a day, it is loud and a little confusing. Voices are competing, the words and tone change and we wonder what they are saying! As the war rages, the call to prayer seems ominous.

We spent another evening texting friends. We are amazed at the supernatural peace and calm we feel in this very volatile situation. Although we never prayed for this peace, it is a gift from God, truly unexplainable to people who are worrying and fearful for us. We are safe and unafraid, while family and friends in the US are nearly paralyzed. I believe I've heard from every person I've ever known, even old high school friends we hadn't heard from in years, were texting. The word is out in America that we are here, and so many are concerned.

Wednesday, October 11, 2023

Mark 7:14-23

"All these evil things proceed from within and defile the man."

Mark 7:23

The Bible explains everything, doesn't it? The heart of man is truly dark until transformed by the Savior's love. All the wickedness we're seeing and hearing about stems from within. The need of the Savior is so very great, but I wonder if people realize their need. All kinds of solutions are offered, but none can offer the forgiveness, power, and redemption but Jesus.

Devotions were led by a staff member this morning, and they were delightful, insightful, and wonderful. Great singing and worship. We are all in this together. There is a new different bond developing that no one expected. We sang our new theme song, You are My Hiding Place again with heartfelt praise to the Lord. The message of that song rings through our minds all day long.

We went back to the apartment for the morning. I wrapped up a sweet roll we'd purchased from the 24/7 Ultra-Orthodox Bakery and put it in the microwave and twirled the knob.

I got distracted and remembered the roll when dark gray smoke filled the kitchen. Oh, no, the microwave was on fire.

Dennis came running into the kitchen and started to open the microwave door. NO…Take it outside. He unplugged it and carried it out to the patio area.

Smoke rolled. But no smoke alarm sounded. Fortunately, that compound wide smoke alarm was being repaired at that very moment and therefore shut off. Thank God for His timing, I would have been so embarrassed. Dennis cleaned the microwave and returned it to the kitchen, I'm sure it's ruined. The smell coming from that oven was awful!

Granddaughter in law, Blakely facetimed us to show us that great grandson Brooks is crawling all over the place. What a delightful distraction. She has no idea of the perfect timing of her call.

Our family members in the states cannot begin to understand how often we think of them and pray for each one specifically. I'm thankful our prayers can reach the One that loves them more than we do. He has the solutions for all their needs.

I guided one group in the afternoon. The Garden Tomb has gained new importance now as the few tourists in Jerusalem are clamoring for the peace that the gospel gives. Tourism has all but vanished. A few straggling groups now stuck in Israel walk from their hotels to get out of their rooms for a bit.

We heard stories of tour groups that had just exited the Ben Gurion airport last Sat. Oct 7th and were left there with no direction or way home. They were on their own. I could not imagine such a difficult situation for those who had saved their money for a long time, planned the details, and were looking forward to this trip.

The director called for a special prayer meeting at 8 p.m. A cross was laid across the huge coffee table in the center of the room. Each one of us was given a torn piece of cloth that represented a concern. After much heartfelt prayer we tied the cloths to the cross and left them there. All concerns were lifted from our hearts and placed on the cross.

We tried to sleep. There were huge rumblings of massive aircraft, helicopters overhead, and gunfire in the streets.

Our Dallas son and daughter-in-law are very concerned and upset. We understand their fear. They are texting our eldest son Andy, and there is a lot of tension, all trying to figure out the best plan. Everyone wants us out of Israel tonight! They are seeing frightening images on American TV that we are not seeing. Our daughter-in-law's dear friend has contacted her brother, who is an ex-Navy seal, who is also involved in one of the evacuation efforts. He will contact us with a plan.

We continue to stress that we truly are safe and unafraid.

We are hearing rumors that all future flights except those operating by EL AL, the Israeli owned airline are cancelled. Dennis stayed up all night searching for seats on El AL.

Every plane owned by EL AL has its own security system. It's my understanding that IF a rocket is fired toward one of their planes, a heat device is fired from the plane itself. The enemy rocket then "searches" for that heat device and destroys it as the plane flies free from harm. What an idea!

We're learning a lot about war.

Thursday, October 12, 2023

Mark 7:24-30

"And she kept asking Him to cast demons out of her daughter."

Mark 7:26

Demons are alive and well and evidently doing their evil work across the land. Stories of terrible acts of violence are still pouring into news agencies. The world has not seen this type of evil since WWII. It is wise to acknowledge the presence and scope of satan and his minions, but unwise to diminish the power of the Almighty God. Greater is He that is in us than he that is in the world.

Our lovely older volunteer brought the morning devotion, stressing the fact that we live in an unclean demonic culture. Jesus is the ONLY answer.

The operations manager is concerned, announcing that all booked flights are now cancelled. We lost hope once again.

Our Dallas friend has booked a ticket to Madrid for next Wednesday.

The pastor and his wife from England are seeking an El Al flight to England ASAP.

Others are continuing to search for flights as well.

The Garden is open today, but very few people are entering. It will be closed tomorrow because Hamas has declared a "day of rage" worldwide. We'll stay inside the gate tomorrow, sheltering in place.

Dennis checked in to Air France. We expect a cancellation for that flight soon. He sent a long e-mail to Andy and Philip, explaining our situation.

We again took the light rail to the Jewish market and IWO. We stocked up on recognizable food, thinking that we would be stranded for quite a while yet.

At 11 a.m., we received notice that the flight on Air France had been cancelled. They suggested refund forms should be filled out. France, Brazil, Poland, and Germany are evacuating their citizens at no cost. No word from the American embassy.

Our ex-Navy Seal friend contacted us again, promising to "get us out." We still have the El AL tickets for next Wednesday. The US State Department notified us that we're on a list, but no further instructions.

Friday, Oct 13, 2023

Mark 7:31-37

"They were utterly astonished, saying, He has done all things well."

Mark 7:37

It's good to remember all the times that Jesus stepped into our lives and did the impossible. Remembering the past strengthens us for today's problems and tomorrow's worries. We can rest in His faithfulness, even when we are faithless!

A Day of Rage! The Garden Gate is closed, and everything is shuttered.

We have four exit options now….El Al next Wednesday, a car trip to Haifa with a promise of a small plane to Cyprus, arranged by Will, the State Department evacuation plane, and the "Save our Allies" plane, Saturday from Ben Gurion.

We visited our Dallas volunteer to discuss all options, thinking that the three of us would exit together eventually. We copied passports and sent them to a woman in Jerusalem who had connections with Glenn Beck's plane, who was promising free flights from Tel Aviv non-stop to Nashville. We sent the passports to "Save our Allies "as well. Uncertainty reigns. Plans change constantly.

We began sorting and packing back at the apartment.

"Saving our Allies" called to check on us. Options are increasing, but so is the confusion and pressure.

We took our turn on the roof, watching for angry Muslim men to march from the Damascus gate to the Garden Tomb gate.

We were told to report any activity so the director could call the military for help.

We learned from the other volunteers that last night, a terrorist shot a policeman at the Damascus Gate, just ½ mile from where we live. The policeman was shot in the leg and will survive. The terrorist was "neutralized" immediately. That explained the helicopters flying low over our heads last night.

We're hearing that the US State Department is preparing to evacuate Americans, but we will have to pay for the flight. (We're wondering about the illegal aliens that get into the southern border of Texas and are flown all over America, providing housing, food, etc., for free. But now is not the time to think of that.)

Our director and his wife prepared a lovely afternoon tea party for the volunteers. It was strange to enjoy such a pleasant gathering knowing that just a few miles away there is carnage taking place in the streets of Gaza. Our leaders are expert at caring for people and we appreciate them deeply.

We received a phone call from our new best friend and ex-Navy Seal and another director from Esther's Journey, another non-profit organization that is helping arrange evacuations. There seems to be many options but no action these days.

Meanwhile I met a young boy in the alley whose hands were full of plastic bags that motioned for me to help him tear his pita bread. I grabbed one side of the flatbread and the other as he ripped it into a smaller size and plopped it into his mouth. Neither of us spoke the other's language but we were joined together in that simple act of his lunch.

We heard through the volunteer grapevine that the UK and the US State Dept. are sending in evacuation planes.

Saturday, October 14, 2023

Mark 8:1-10

"I feel compassion for the people."

Mark 8:2

As much as our heart breaks for the people who have suffered so greatly these past few days, we know that Jesus is very well aware of their pain as well. He knows pain, He knows rejection, He knows humiliation, and He knows death.

He also knows that believers will be resurrected one day to enjoy Him forever.

We learned at devotions this morning that two children were shot dead in the streets outside our gate last night. We sang, we prayed, we read the scriptures.

And our director announced, "It's time to flee."

He has spoken with the authorities in Jerusalem and the Garden Tomb board of directors back in the UK.

The board decided that even though everyone was confident that the Lord would take care of us all, it was time for everyone to evacuate. They used the passage of scripture where the angel told Joseph to take Mary and the baby to "flee to Egypt." Couldn't the Heavenly Father have protected and cared for them? Is there a time to stand and wait, and also another time to flee?

A few volunteers expressed their desire to stay at the Garden regardless of the danger, strongly believing that no matter what might come the Lord would protect us all. After prayer all agreed to abide by the Board of Directors wishes.

No one at the Garden Tomb is to be martyred at this point in time. Everyone should make immediate plans to go home, wherever home might be.

The Garden Tomb Gate will be closed. Everyone was sad.

Shortly after devotions, we got a text from our ex-Navy Seal friend, "Get ready to leave" in the next few hours. There would be a plane at Tel Aviv to take us either to Frankfurt, Germany, or Athens, Greece, and he was sure our names were on the manifest.

I explained to him that we needed some time to get to the airport. He urged us to "stand by."

A group of tourists from California appeared at the gate. Dennis volunteered to give them a tour of the property. The normal 20-minute tour lasted 2 hours as they stopped and held worship services at every turn. It was phenomenal. When he arrived back at the gate we took a picture with volunteers and staff and Dennis, proclaiming him to be the guide with the "longest tour" in the history of the Garden. So many smiles and so much love. Again, supernatural peace is found in this place where the Lord is praised.

At 3 p.m., we received another text. All it said was,
"GO NOW"

We told the staff member and our beloved friend this news, and he calmly stated, "I'll have a van for you at the gate in 15 minutes."

We raced to our apartment and started throwing things into suitcases. We left piles of shoes, clothes, and anything we wouldn't need in the next few days on the living room coffee table.

What to do with the bacon? At $50 a pound, it was a priceless commodity. We decided to "bequeath" it to our bacon-loving Scottish volunteer. Those left behind will enjoy that treat.

We carried our suitcases down the two flights of outdoor stairs to the front gate where we were met by other volunteers. They were giving us a sendoff. Everyone who wasn't busy arrived and offered tight hugs and big tears. We were the first ones to leave.

When would we see these precious friends again? What would happen to them in the next few days? What would happen to us? The van appeared.

Our Jewish driver spoke no English, the van door slid closed, and we were off.

There were no cars on the streets or highways, and we knew we were not on the usual route to Tel Aviv. Nothing was familiar.

A checkpoint appeared with a young Israeli soldier carrying an AK-47 peering into the window of the van. We waved our blue passports and he let us by.

Our ex-Navy Seal texted, "Where are you? We need to know where you are in case we need to rescue you."

WHAT? I saw NO danger anywhere, and we were almost to the airport.

We texted back, "We don't know where we are, there are no cars anywhere on the road and the driver doesn't speak English."

We later learned that this road was the alternative to the main drive to the airport because, in past experiences, snipers were positioned along that main road.

He texted again...."Where are you?"

Another check point appeared. We knew the drill. After our driver spoke to the military people the van door slid open and we waved our blue American passports again.

We were sent through.

There were still no cars on the road. It was a very bizarre scene. This road normally would have been filled with traffic, both tourists and locals.

He texted again. We answered, "We are approaching the airport," and shut off the phone.

The driver drove right up to the front door and let us out. We breathed a sigh of relief.

Surely we were on our way home.

Very near the entrance, we saw the US Embassy staff. They all had yellow vests and stood near the American flag. What a beautiful sight.

We checked in with them, signed a paper saying we might be charged for this flight in the future, and were told to sit nearby and wait for them to call our names.

We had been seated for about 10 minutes when the air raid sirens started wailing. We knew the sound, and we knew what to do.

I ran to a nearby wall and fell down flat on the floor, covering my head with my hands. I examined the tile floor close up, and as I looked up, I saw Dennis standing near our bags, looking perplexed. Thousands of others were also lying on the ground. The sirens continued, and I felt the building shake. The rockets being fired were intercepted by the Israeli Iron Dome Missile Defense Program. The bombs truly were bursting in the air.

After 10 minutes, everyone around me started getting up, going back to their chairs to wait.

We were safe and still unafraid.

Later, an embassy official waved a flag and shouted out, "Will 60 Americans follow me?"

We formed a ragged line and followed the flag through the airport.

He took us to a ticket counter, where he told us to line up. We would be getting a boarding pass to ATHENS, GREECE.

Suddenly, the ticket counter agent refused his request. She stated, 'No, we have a flight to check in before you. Your group will wait.' Our embassy friend left us with no explanation or direction.

We waited, along with hundreds of folks milling about. There was great confusion.

Finally, an hour later, the ticket agent motioned for our group to step up to the counter.

We were toward the front of the line, so we were issued our boarding pass, and they placed our luggage on the conveyor belt. Yes, we were headed to Athens, Greece, and the time of departure on the boarding pass was 7:15 p.m. Since it was already past 8 p.m., we were confused once again.

We followed the line through another check point. Our passports were opened and laid down upon a screen. After approval, the single gate opened and Dennis walked through. My passport was refused. After many tries, I flagged down an airport employee, and he directed me over to another machine. He opened my Passport, laid it down and bingo, the gate flew open for me, too.

We walked through the airport corridors toward the boarding gates. Hundreds of families, crying babies, and very tired children were packed into the waiting area.

At 9:30, the rockets lit up the skies right outside the terminal windows. Everyone started running back into the terminal away from the windows. The building shook, and the airport was under attack again. We heard the explosions in the air as the Iron Dome once again intercepted rockets.

How could an airplane possibly land in this situation?

I got tired of running so found a wall to slide down to the floor to sit and watch the running parade go by me. What a bizarre scene.

Soon, people started walking slowly back to the windows and the waiting area. Oh, so many people who didn't look American. And I realized several airlines from other countries were also going to board passengers at nearby gates, but no matter the nationalities we were all in this together.

Babies were screaming, and everyone's nerves were on edge. It seemed like we were living inside a movie set.

Andy texted, "Mom, what are you going to do once you get to Athens?" Well, I never thought about that. He put us in touch with his pastor friend who lived there and whose church had a guest house. He would pick us up at the airport and deliver us to the guest house.

A few minutes later, Philip texted. "Mom, what are you going to do once you get to Athens?"

I shared with him our plan. He replied, "No, get yourself to the Four Seasons Resort, you are registered there. Check in and stay as long as you want. Take advantage of everything that resort has to offer, and stay as long as you want, you have no budget."

WHAT? I spoke with the Greek pastor and told him of the offer. He excitedly proclaimed, "By all means, go to the Four Seasons." I thanked him profusely and promised to visit him and his lovely wife the next time we were in Athens.

We waited and waited, stunned by the whole situation. Peace for us in the midst of unbelievable chaos, where peace did not reign in the eyes of our fellow refugees.

Finally, a plane rolled up to the gate nearest us. It was plain white, with no markings at all, and it was not registered on the departure billboard in the terminal. This plane was "under the radar."

Sunday, October 15, 2023

We were told boarding would begin immediately. We waited in line, boarded, and sat down with a sigh. It was 12:15 a.m. We decided the plane had been leased from an Asian country. The seats were very tiny, and the flight attendants were Asian. This was NOT an American plane.

The State Department had arranged this evacuation, and we were very thankful.

We texted our grown children and told them we were onboard. We could hear THEIR sigh of relief from across the world.

Dennis was cautious. He said, "We can breathe easily when we get to 10K feet, above the range of the rockets."

The plane took off, we were in the air, and soon we were above 10K, exhausted and breathing.

Two hours later, we landed in Greece and were directed to a bus that would take us to the terminal. We waited at baggage claim, and Dennis's bag was the very last one to appear.

We texted the kids again that we had safely landed in Greece.

An elderly Russian man stood alone and needed help. He spoke no English or Greek and was clearly very confused. We tried to explain to him where he was and what he should do next. We finally found an airport employee who could communicate with him, and we were out the door.

We felt profound sorrow for so many folks that were displaced, perplexed and without any plan of what to do or where to go next.

We found a taxi outside the terminal (2:30 a.m.), and the driver assured us in broken English that he knew where the Four Seasons was located. After a 20-minute Drive, we arrived at the most beautiful, stunning resort we'd ever seen. Even in the dark, we decided it was truly heaven. We collapsed in a bed of comfort and slept until 9:30 a.m. Sunday, October 15, 2023.

The next day, we ate lunch at the resort and marveled at the blue sea, the landscape, the beautiful people, the stunning buildings, the pools, the décor, the ships in the harbor, the children playing in the sand, the drinks with little umbrellas, the magnificent food options, and the absence of Air Raid Sirens and bombs exploding.

We slept the day away.

Monday, October 16, 2023
Mark 8 and 9.

All my notes for teaching these passages in Mark were somewhere in my luggage. Next time!

Monday morning, at 6 a.m., I woke up to a severe sore throat. I'd been so very careful to pray for good health and energy, knowing I would be in all kinds of situations beyond my control. Dennis was struggling with United Airlines at that early hour, trying to get a flight from Athens to America, but they would not change our flight from Paris, scheduled for Wednesday. He was so frustrated. There was a direct flight from Athens to the US, but they refused to accommodate us even after explaining that we'd just be evacuated from Israel by the State Dept. and we had no control over where they took us. He finally arranged a short flight from Athens to Paris so we could catch that United flight home to DC. We'll never fly United again.

I felt like razor blades lined my throat all down my esophagus. We called the hotel to see if they could recommend a doctor nearby. Dr. George T. arrived at our door within the hour. He prescribed an antibiotic that was delivered 45 minutes later. Praise God for the Four Seasons staff! Dr. T was an elderly, sophisticated gentleman who had worked for the resort for many years. Evidently, he was the hotel doctor who came to the rescue of foreigners like us.

We watched the news in that lovely, very safe room. It was so very depressing and so slanted against Israel. Even though Hamas terrorists had slaughtered, tortured women, children, babies, and kidnapped over 250 hostages, it seemed the world was demanding that they do nothing in response.

The Jewish mantra "Never Again" was happening.

We contacted our friends at the Garden Tomb. Plans were being made staff and volunteers would trickle out of Israel and back to their homes by next week. The gate would be closed and the garden would be empty.

How things have changed! Instead of preparing and greeting thousands of scheduled visitors, all tours are cancelled.

Meanwhile, we headed out to tour Athens. The people at the resort drove us by golf cart to a place where we could board the "on/off bus," and there we waited. We met another couple that had been evacuated from Israel, an elderly Jewish couple from Florida. We boarded together for a day of sightseeing. The traffic was horrible, and the bus ride was long. We could see the Acropolis from a distance and made arrangements with Christina, Demetri's wife, to meet her on Tuesday for a private tour of this amazing city. We finally gave up on the "on/off bus" and took a cab back to the resort.

The Jewish couple exited the bus at the same time, but refused to join us in the cab because "it was too expensive, $70. The cab driver brushed him off, "he's Jewish, they're all alike." Here it is again! Anti-Semitism is alive and well in Greece! And I wonder what happened to that little couple, alone in such a big city. Where were all those people who had been evacuated?

We spoke with our Dallas volunteer friend back at the Garden Tomb, who was still trying to get on the Save Our Allies plane. It was rescheduled again. That was very frustrating for him, so he decided to take a flight to Madrid; he'd be leaving at 1 a.m. the next morning. We arrived back at the resort just in time for a hair appointment! What a delightful experience and the best haircut of my life, it was desperately needed. But even a new hairdo didn't help the sore throat and extreme fatigue. I was getting sicker by the moment.

After dinner at one of the lovely resort restaurants, we collapsed again for blessed sleep.

Tuesday, October 17, 2023

We cancelled plans for the city tour with the Greek Pastor's wife. I am just too sick to even try to go into the city. We decided to relax the day away at the resort. Following brunch at the Mercata, we strolled the grounds and enjoyed the sunshine. More naps.

It was another day of sore throat and fatigue. We found a cabana by the water and sat there all afternoon. I need to get well quickly! We are still far away from home. The wait staff checked on us from time to time and brought us everything we needed. We ate dinner at a Mexican place by the water, sitting at a small table in the sand. Could it get any lovelier?

This rest was desperately needed.

Wednesday, October 18, 2023

Sleep, blessed sleep. We rode the golf cart to the Mucata for breakfast and returned to pack up for our flight to Paris. A taxi took us to the airport at about 10:30 a.m., and we boarded the plane at about 2 p.m. The Aegean Airlines plane was packed with a large group of men being "relocated?" At 4:30, we were in the air to Paris. We learned via texting that two English volunteers had left the Garden Tomb for the UK, and our Dallas friend was on his way to Madrid. The English pastor and his wife are home but "jumpy." They told friends not to call and that they needed some time alone and would let them know when they were ready to tell their tale. The aftershocks of this experience are real for so many. The Garden Tomb staff member told us that everyone would be evacuated by Sunday.

We played chess on the little set I'd packed in my carry-on, ate sandwiches we brought on the plane, but our minds were filled with concern for the people that were left behind. So many locals that had nowhere to go but to their homes in the war zone. Praying.

We prayed for PEACE, begging the Prince of Peace to intervene in this terrible situation.

The plane landed in Paris and we exited to the very large terminal and more people. We finally found the tram that would take us to the exit nearest our hotel. The hotel people promised that they were located right outside the door.

We got off the tram and walked through the door to a cold, rainy evening. By now, Dennis's suitcase had only three wheels and we could see the hotel sign in the sky, about a ½ mile away. Yes, we were the lonely old people limping through the rain, dragging our luggage down a rugged street. We arrived about 6:30 p.m., found our room and waited for the restaurant to open at 7. After dinner we collapsed in our bed.

At 10 p.m., the hotel fire alarm sounded. Was that an Air Raid Siren? We joined other confused guests dressed in their pajamas in the hotel hallway and began the long trip down the stairs to the outside. Still raining, we all stood looking for the flames that must be shooting from the hotel roof. No flames, no smoke. Finally, we made our way to the front entrance and desk along with many other sleepy vagabonds. The manager declared that all was well, a guest had been smoking in bed, and that triggered the fire alarm. It was safe to go back to bed.

How can all this be happening? We climbed the stairs and once again fell into bed.

Thursday, October 19, 2023

The shuttle was waiting outside the hotel at 6:30 a.m. to take us and others to the Charles DE Gaulle airport. The check in was horrendous. Their IT system was down and we waited in line with thousands of people for it to be rebooted. We prayed. We will arrive at Washington D.C. with minutes to spare before boarding the Southwest flight to Dallas.

We heard from our Garden Tomb friends. All have been evacuated but the barebones staff members.

After the machines began working again, they would not accept my passport. After several attempts, I contacted an airport employee who helped. Entering the main part of the terminal was magical. High-end stores lined the walkways, Prada, Gucci, etc. Oh, my….it was a sight to behold. I took pictures of the glitzy shopping area but bought nothing. Anything they had to offer seemed ridiculous as I remembered our friends still heading to bomb shelters back in Jerusalem.

We finally boarded the plane at about 12:30 p.m., and the plane taxied out of the gate area. The pilot spoke over the loudspeaker, we would be returning to the gate to retrieve a food cart that had mistakenly been left behind. We taxied back to the gate, and an HOUR later, the plane was positioned for takeoff.

Eight long hours of flight to Washington, D.C. We arrived at 3:55 pm US time and our flight to Dallas was to leave at 5:05.

The flight crew asked everyone that did NOT have a connecting flight to stay seated and let those people off first. Of course, no one stayed seated and another long wait began.

Entering and leaving customs was another nightmare, but we finally got our bags to re-check to Dallas. We had 25 minutes to get to D terminal. It was 2 miles away.

We took off in a dead run. This sick old woman arrived as the door was about to close.

A flight attendant was standing at the front of the plane holding a tray of glasses of water.

I panted, "I'm 80 years old and just ran 2 miles, I need that water." He quickly handed it to me and I drank it down. As I walked down the aisle the people in the first class seats started clapping for me. All smiles and well wishes, "You did great for an old lady." I was shocked, why did I tell that attendant I was 80 years old? Delirious I suppose.

We fell into our seats for the flight to Dallas and arrived at 7:15 p.m. Our Dallas son and his beautiful wife picked us up at the curb. (It was their wedding anniversary.) What a beautiful sight, how we missed them! We hugged a long time before loading up for dinner and home.

At the house, I did a little dance in our driveway, proclaiming my love for my front door, the garage door, the windows of the house, the trees, and the driveway. We all laughed and cried together. Another family member left food in the fridge and flowers on the counter. Welcome home. What a sweet thing to do. We collapsed in our own bed for the first time since September 1st.

Friday, October 20, 2023

We relaxed and smiled all day today and went to granddaughter Mollie's evening volleyball game at Highland Park. It was such a normal thing to do. Normal was a welcome experience.

They won.

After hugs and pictures with the Dallas grands we settled into our home once again. Tomorrow would be another day to go to the Dr. for American meds.

Saturday, October 21, 2023
Our 52nd wedding anniversary.

A few days later, we met with Dallas Garden Tomb volunteers and heard of his exit from Israel. He was driven to Ben Gurion airport by a Palestinian driver. They were stopped twice in the middle of the night at check points. A soldier pointed his AK47 at him demanding his passport. He arrived late to Madrid and missed his flight to the US so he had to stay in a hotel there, $400. What an experience for him! Every volunteer leaving Jerusalem had a story.

Four staff members were still in Jerusalem at that time with plans to leave in a couple of days, and the gate would be closed indefinitely.

Staff members who live in or near Jerusalem will check on the Garden regularly. They will sing praise songs in that empty place and post their worship services online. Two cats will be fed, weeds will be pulled, and many prayers will be uttered for the people suffering so terribly just a few miles away. The war rages on.

End of January 2024

The director of the Garden Tomb and his wife returned from England to Jerusalem and opened the gate!

A skeleton staff returned later in February.

Tourists began trickling in, but the war raged on.

That quiet place of prayer and reflection, the oasis in the midst of chaos, offered peace and the gospel of Jesus Christ to all who entered, and it is open once again. HIS truth is again being proclaimed, even in a war zone.

Tourists are few, and the citizens of the country who rely on their funds are suffering terribly. Jobs are rare, young men and women are engaged in battle in the south and north of Israel, borders are sealed, food is scarce, and prejudices are alive and well. Death tolls are rising, and hope seems all but lost that hostages will be freed. Many have been killed.

This war is being witnessed by the entire globe. It is a battle raging against the God of the Universe and the evil one. God's people, His promises, and His very character are being threatened. The world is taking sides, and history is being repeated.

The end will be the same as in the past days. God wins, He always wins. His plans for His people will not be thwarted and He is not surprised by anything we are seeing. His promises stand firm.

His Supernatural presence can be experienced by anyone who calls upon His name with a sincere heart of surrender to His will.

We've learned that peace is not determined by outward circumstances, by our own worth or pitiful deeds of holiness, but by the faithfulness of God who has promised to "never leave you or forsake you, until the end of the age." His presence is a Supernatural gift, He alone is worthy to be praised in all circumstances of this life.

End of February 2024

We received a bill from the US State Department. Our flight from Tel Aviv to Athens, normally a short hop, costs $100. per ticket. We were to pay $358. Each in 30 days, or our Social Security would be affected, there would be fines, late fees, and the IRS would be involved. I contacted several Congressmen, the Governor, national reporters, and people at the State Dept. No one had the power to do anything about this price gouging, but they offered their sympathy. That's the way it is in America these days. Underlings define procedures that have nothing to do with the law.

Will we return to East Jerusalem, Israel? Yes. Will we return to the Garden Tomb Site? Yes. Either there or here in the United States, we will forever proclaim that Jesus Christ is the Son of the Living God, that He lived a righteous life and died a horrible death for the payment of the sins of mankind. Whoever receives that free gift of salvation by His grace can know His supernatural peace. Forgiveness and reconciliation with the Heavenly Father change everything! We've experienced the Peace of God and the Peace with God. And His supernatural peace confirms the promise of Matthew 28:20b, "I am with you always, even to the end of the world."

We are confident in every situation because,

"I am convinced that <u>neither death, nor life</u>, nor angels, nor principalities, nor things present, nor things to come, nor powers, nor height, nor depth, nor any other created thing, will be able to separate us from the love of God, which is in Christ Jesus our Lord."

Romans 8:38-39

www.ingramcontent.com/pod-product-compliance
Lightning Source LLC
LaVergne TN
LVHW051035070526
838201LV00009B/202